Dr Alexander Cannon

Dr Cannon's psychic assistants

Rhonda de Rhonda (left) and Joyce de Rhonda (right)

*'The empires of the future will be
the empires of the mind'*

Winston Churchill, September 6th 1943

1

*It was not immediately apparent why a semi-naked man was lying
in a distressed state on a rickety old battlefield camp bed erected in
a dark shed-like structure. Strange it was indeed that the row of
sheds stood in the yard of a grand residence in the countryside. The
household staff wondered briefly; they gawped through the kitchen
window. They had heard and seen it all before.*

*A flimsy blanket flapped around him, pretty useless in the
character-building cold. He had fitted himself into the bed like a
sardine in a can, as though fearing an electric shock if a limb should
stray across the edge. He muttered and mumbled, then shouted out
loud, his brain full of Arctic hell, logistical cock-ups, and the names
of men who had drowned unreported. There had been a need for
propaganda spin to gloss over the worst failures. He pondered these
things as he lay in a strange silvery light. The whiteness of his skinny*

torso seemed luminous, as did the white circles around his eyes, contrasting with his sunburnt cheeks and neck, and his jet black beard.

But then he returned to the task in hand, and as he did so, his breathing slowed. He did what he was being told to do to calm himself – breathe deeply. At the end of his bed stood a wind-up gramophone from which the voice of a hypnotist boomed: 'Every day, in every way, you're feeling better... stronger... younger... you shall overcome... thou shalt overcome that which needs to be overcome... Fear is proof of a degenerate mind...'

The slow pace and the commanding voice was like that of an evangelical American preacher with exaggerated, elongated endings of sentences. But the accent was English, with northern flashes.

The only light in the room came from the unusual silvery blue bulb which barely lifted the darkness of black-painted walls. And to call it a room is an exaggeration. It was more like a wooden lean-to, attached to the back of the large house, his belongings piled onto the bare concrete floor where a hint of moss remained. This man was no Ordinary Joe: plenty of cash, some ration coupons; a business card from Mirabelle's restaurant in Mayfair, where our man bumped into acquaintances such as film star David Niven and the Duke of Windsor, as Edward VIII was rebranded after the abdication. Also in the pile of possessions were gent's club membership cards. A silver Rolex watch glistening in the blue light.

At the head of the bed was an instrument which would look at home in Frankenstein's laboratory – a Wimshurst electro-static generator – two white spinning wheels just a couple of inches apart. At intervals similar to the numbers on a clock face, flat pads were wired to the centre of the wheels, which themselves were at least a couple of feet in diameter. Two soft pads connected by a clamp looked like crude headphones which were themselves attached to the machine with thick cabling. If this machine had played a part in triggering his distress, you could understand 'how' at least, perhaps not 'why'.

His listening was interrupted. He had tuned into the wheezy engine of the local pharmacist's delivery van, then to the sound of the wind and surf at the beach not too far away. And then for him the best sound of all, the unmistakable roar of a Spitfire coming in to land on the airstrip very close by. These sounds calmed him as he remembered that life went on.

The van tootling through the countryside was marked with the name of a pharmacy – Quirk's Chemist of Ramsey – and it was heading in bright sun towards the house, and to the RAF base at Jurby next door, in the north of the Isle of Man. There were deliveries also to cottages near a small chapel whose doors and gravestones bore Celtic symbols. The Manx flag flew high on flagpoles in front gardens and the cemetery.

A loud change of gear signalled a left turn down the long tree-lined drive to the house which the new 'come-over' owner insisted should be called a 'castle'. Islanders laughed at, but quietly went along with, his pretensions, but the imperial grandeur did match such a description. A clutch of palm trees formed a turning circle in the middle of the gravel in front of the impressive sandstone archway over the front door.

Intrigue surrounding the property had recently increased because of the bizarre new owner. He had popped up from nowhere and moved in at the start of the war. Then, towards the end of 1940, fighter planes were based next to the long acres of his garden, some of them tucked under the canopies of his trees just in case the Germans carried out any reconnaissance. The RAF commanders and other 'high-ups' appeared to be close to this intriguing man – a doctor who looked more like a circus ringmaster, what with his big smiling face and his weird entourage.

The lonely patient meanwhile listened from his shed at the rear of the house to the gravel crunch of Mr Quirk's arrival at the side door. Not blessed with any sun on his frozen skin, our man diverted himself by studying the little silver stars which had been painted on the black ceiling. He could make out the door bell ring in the distance. Perhaps that nice Mr Quirk would bring a welcome tranquiliser in his tray of tablets and bottles of folic acid.

And then the curtain was flung open and the sun streamed in along with an exotically-dressed, remarkably beautiful young woman who knelt down next to the camp bed. He smiled as she threw her arms round him – her hour glass figure accentuated by an outfit which looked like it was from the best shops in London. She had to kneel awkwardly on the concrete floor, her legs gripped together by a tight pencil skirt. Our man's hand caressed her perfectly formed behind while she stroked his beard and kissed him with all her might. His hand was slightly wrinkly, his beard made him look even older than he was. Her skin was perfect. She looked, and in fact was, young enough to be his daughter.

When she spoke, it was with a wooden, upper crust Brief Encounter accent: 'Poor Geoffrey! Doctor says that terrible time in Norway is still left inside you.' They looked like they were in love.

Watching them from the door, peering in to the shed where our couple embraced, was the big man himself – 'the Doctor'. He had a large bald head and ruddy complexion, was dressed in Victorian *garb, with bat wing collar and cravat, a cloak and cane, black and white spats on his feet. He took a few strides forward to make his presence known, and our cooing couple cooed no more. The woman stood to attention, brushing herself down, but there was no doubt that 'Doctor' was more than happy to see how well they were getting on. He had good reason to be pleased. But the reason for his pleasure was an official secret.*

2

It seems appropriate to start this story with an imagined scene from the everyday life of Dr Alexander Cannon. It breathes life into one day, one moment, in this uber-weird story of the occultist who was also a properly-qualified doctor. Britain's Rasputin, you could say. At first, the basic facts about Dr Cannon were what caught my imagination. I never expected to go on to assemble a very large jigsaw of information over a number of years. Names and events referred to in history books, archives and journals began to fall into place with facts spelt out in Dr Cannon's secret service files, and in interviews with the very few people still alive who had met the man.

Two great qualities of this slice of Britain's secret history are that it is so remarkable, and that it is as true as I can get it.

I might have embellished the drama with the quivering commander in the shed, but only a little. There was talk of Cannon being involved in wartime brain-washing experiments; he was definitely involved in experiments in the paranormal.

It is absolutely true that patients drawn from the top brass of the military during the war really did fly to the Isle of Man Clinic for Nervous Disorders for post-traumatic stress 'treatments', and to take part in the weird experiments. Some of them were commandos and naval admirals just in from raids on Europe's Nazi-occupied coastline. Cannon told them – and anyone else who would listen – about his secret connections with the royal family, and how he treated King George VI for his stammer and nicotine addiction. But they laughed behind his back at his lies.

It is also true that two women at the clinic who helped to 'treat' patients were real-life psychic sisters who came to be dominated by Cannon, the younger was a Jane Fonda lookalike. The silver-starred 'therapy sheds' at the rear of a grand residence on the Isle of Man really did exist – Dr Cannon believed in electrical stimulation and its significance in enhancing the brain's 'psychic' activity.

The full story of exactly who believed in him, and what the doctor got up to in the 1930s and 1940s, is truly remarkable.

3

I got on to the tale of Dr Cannon some years ago. One afternoon, my dad who lives on the Isle of Man phoned to tell me a file had found its way into the Manx Museum archive. It was an MI5 file discovered at the back of a filing cabinet. It had Manx police reports mixed in as well. Agents and officers had been watching and spying on this man who claimed the titles 'His Excellency' Dr 'Sir' Alexander Cannon.

Dr Cannon had once given a magic demonstration for my dad's school science club on the island in the 1950s, a performance involving a mystery voice booming from behind stage curtains, crashing cymbals making my dad and his school mates laugh out loud. When 'doctor' emerged in his cloak and top hat, stumbling around in dry ice, muffled giggles gave way to loud laughter. But Dr Cannon soldiered on regardless.

Thinking about it, the record my dad listened to at The Enchanted Hall, Dr Cannon's private mini-theatre, was probably from the same batch as the ones played in the 'therapy sheds'. Back then as my dad told me the little he knew, the details of the sheds and the grand house were unknown to me. All my dad and I knew were the basics – that for some reason, MI5 watched a man called Dr Alexander Cannon very closely and tried to control him. He appeared to be a 'loose cannon' but no-one knew why he was apparently so dangerous. There had been talk of him being a Nazi spy – he was hypnotising the top brass of the military. They had details in their heads of some of the most sensitive operations of the war.

Some weeks after dad's phone call, I had a complete copy of the file. A Manx Museum archivist had posted me photocopies section by section. As each instalment arrived on the door mat, my fascination grew.

On the Isle of Man, the doctor provoked gossip from the start of the Second World War until he died in 1963. My grandmother knew about him. He was a classic 'dooiney quaagh' (pron: dun-yah qw-air-kgh), which in the island's own Celtic language of Manx means 'weirdo'.

Dr Cannon was definitely a 'dooiney quaagh'. Had the file been discovered in London, I wondered if it would have been snaffled quietly away. I like to believe that would have been the case. Discovered in the Isle of Man, it made its way into a public archive which no-one knew about, and it was fascinating reading.

4

Opposite my dad's house on the island lived Percy Cowley. He used the stage name Salamander throughout the war years. His stage act included the Indian rope trick, and lying on a bed of nails dressed only in a turban and a loin cloth; he steered clear of darkening his skin with gravy browning for extra effect. Percy was in his 80s when I spoke to him in mid-2006, when he told me of his performances on stage with Cannon in the 1950s in the so-called Enchanted Hall, which the doctor had built in the grounds of his third home on the Isle of Man, Laureston Manor in Douglas.

At such shows, Cannon was known for a number of tricks, each performed with great pomp. One involved an airtight coffin and "a message from the other side". The doctor-cum-magician seemed unaware the audience was laughing *at* rather than *with* him, as he emerged from the coffin after a half hour incarceration to read out his message. Occasionally he was heckled by members of the audience, especially during shows at Onchan village hall. One time, he emerged from the coffin and asked to be handed a piece of paper he admitted he had forgotten to take with him. Unabashed, he read his message from beyond. True to his home county of Yorkshire, this man was brass-necked for sure.

In his latter years, movement was difficult for Cannon who, despite being a doctor, had undiagnosed diabetes for years, and so both his legs had to be amputated. He walked using tin legs.

Two women, his assistants, share a graveyard plot with him in a small cemetery in Onchan, overlooking Douglas bay, just around the corner from the village hall. Were they the two psychic sisters? The three of them had died within a period of ten years. What else had he shared with them?

Percy had been luke warm about talking to me when I telephoned ahead to say who I was and why I was coming. But I went in any case.

He shouted from the lounge for me to come in through the unlocked front door (normal on the Isle of Man) to his house which stank of cigarette smoke. I walked in to the front room, and there he was. This emaciated old man sat in an armchair in the middle of the room – the chair was almost the solitary item of furniture except for a TV and a round metal ashtray on a stand which looked like a flamingo leg and a claw at its base, a hint of his holiday resort show-biz past. The ash tray was bursting with tab ends. He was a minor medical miracle – chain smoking and apparently alive and alert and heading towards his ninetieth year. Percy's arms lay on special arm rests, and there was little expression on his face. Percy stubbed out one cigarette and simultaneously lit another. He was dressed in a smart suit, shirt and tie, which overwhelmed his tired old body. He was not going to make this interview easy. I found myself stumbling around trying to justify my reasons for investigating Dr Cannon's story: "Did you think he was a spy?"

The rumours about Dr Cannon were complex. My grandmother talked of 'those poor women' who had fallen under his control. Some who knew more detail spoke of his incredible – and risible – scientific claims, his close connections with royalty and Winston Churchill, and suspicions that he was a German spy.

Percy would only say he was aware that Dr Cannon had lots of secrets, he had great difficulties during the war – men in suits would come and go, admirals, commanders and the well-to-do – his clinic was top secret, but Percy knew no further detail, and then even what he did know was probably not true. The secrets had gone to his grave; Cannon was a tease and there was nothing more to tell. Everything he said was probably a lie. He took a drag on his cigarette. He guided his hand carefully back towards the armchair, flicking the ash into the tray on its way down. That was that.

I felt I was overstaying my welcome, but when I expressed an interest in his showbiz magic performances over the decades, we were off. Percy became animated. He leant forward and pulled a box around from the side of his armchair. The box and its yellowed contents were decades old, covered in salt crystals from damp brickwork.

He brushed off the salt sediment as he told me he had got the box from the cellar when I rang him earlier in the day. He explained his life as a performer and the contents of the box.

They were scrap books containing personal letters to Salamander from someone who signed himself Lord Strange; a 1969 programme of "A Night of Mystery and Magic – in memory of Dr Sir Alexander Cannon – at The Enchanted Hall, Laureston Manor, Douglas"; lots of 1950s newspaper cuttings with photographs of a much younger, semi-naked Salamander sporting a hairy chest and a turban and a sword, standing next to a row of embarrassed town councillors; a publicity photograph of a 1960s multiple poodle stage act, The Wychwoods – in the picture, a leggy, busty, slim blonde woman with a coiffeured poodle under her arm cuddled up to her comedy frumpy husband. A message penned in biro on the back of the photo: "To Percy, My secret lover…love Audrey." Percy looked up at me, his mind elsewhere, a big beaming smile across his face.

In amongst the scrap books, six boxes contained reel-to-reel tapes and gramophone records, all of them recordings of Dr Cannon speaking at the Enchanted Hall and elsewhere. And then there were water-damaged books by Cannon which were barely salvageable:

The Powers Within; *The Invisible Influence;* and the 8mm film of The Coffin and The Message from Beyond trick.

Percy picked up the box. "Here, you take them. I have no use for them now. Cannon would have liked you to have them. He wants you to tell his story, I am sure of that."

5

The discovery of a dusty old MI5 file at the back of a filing cabinet was what had set me on a ferry to see my dad, then to Percy Cowley, and then on a drive to the north of the Isle of Man.

I stopped my car to look up the tree-lined driveway to what might have been a minor chateau in France. My children's protests that I was embarrassing them yet again were soon drowned out by the sound of gravel crunching under our tyres. One look at the house and they too were finally hooked by the mystery of Dr Cannon. Only on bank holiday trips or on the telly had they seen or been in houses like this. And then the very posh owner was helping them out of the car and taking them into what she says used to be the scullery. Mrs Pamela Shimwell, who bought the house in the early 1960s, was delighted that someone was finally investigating Dr Cannon, and delighted at how fascinated the kids were.

She was full of stories about him I had heard from others: his claims to have advised the royal family and Churchill: "He was the most incredible liar, the most bizarre man, dominating any room he was in. But he was clearly very intelligent."

There were still odd Cannon remnants in her massive barn of a garage where a vintage car stood under a tarpaulin. She picked up a framed photograph from a workbench. There was Dr Cannon on the back row for his final year Leeds University group photograph with fellow medical students in the summer of 1924, the year he became a fully-qualified doctor. We stood in silence and looked at it; we agreed that the expression on his face, in particular the smirk of a smile, was "perhaps sinister... definitely smug". We both laughed politely.

The blacked out room, or the 'therapy shed', was one of a row of six or maybe seven which were knocked down a few decades ago. Tiny traces are still visible of the wood and nails which attached them to the external rear walls of the house. I had a slightly clearer picture in my mind of what had gone on in the early 1940s. Mrs Shimwell is well informed about some aspects of this story, the treatment sheds, or rooms, as she called them.

She described what she found when she moved in during the very early 1960s: in the row of rooms, which must have been freezing most of the year, rotting wooden battlefield camp beds and bits of civilian debris inside; nearby, a mini-electrical generator had ensured the power supply 'no matter what happened, even if the Germans had invaded'; the books, the Far Eastern trinket he gave her as a wedding present, and one or two gramophone records scattered around and abandoned. They were authored and voiced by the man who sold her the house, Dr Alexander Cannon.

6

A newsroom Christmas party hangover fogged my head early one Saturday morning. It was December 2006, 70 years after the abdication, almost to the day.

On the radio, Perry Como's *Christmas Dream*, the ultimate in 1960s schmaltz. It even has a children's choir singing in real

Christmassy *Deutsch*. The song set off a train of thought which as it turned out was appropriate to the day. It is the theme to the *Odessa File*, a film released in 1974, starring Jon Voigt as a journalist who stumbles across a file listing war criminals re-assimilated into West German society. Voight uses the file to track down a bunch of old Nazis. I remembered watching the film in the 1980s and hoping that one day, I too would be such a journalist handed a file which would allow me to track down a bunch of old Nazis. I hoped for my own Odessa file moment, some crucial evidence falling into my lap which would unravel a story about nasty people who should be in prison, but were not.

The Odessa File theme tune *Christmas Dream* and its words were on a loop in my head: *Watch me now, here I go, all I need's a little snow…* There was a chance that this Hangover Saturday could turn into Odessa File Day, the moment where I would be handed a cracking tale. I had already been handed part of a file. Now I hoped more digging would reap greater results.

For earlier that week, a man had telephoned me. The Daily Telegraph had followed up a story of mine based on the Cannon file, just days before the actual 70th anniversary of the abdication, on December 10th 1936. He had seen the story.

It had been published that week: the strange tale of the Yorkshireman who claimed fraudulent titles and who had treated King Edward VIII in the run-up to the abdication crisis for drink problems, using hypnotic and occult-type methods. There were said to be sexual problems too.

Dr Cannon's clinic had back in 1936 been on Harley Street, just a few doors down from Lionel Logue's practice, another royal quack who treated King George VI for his stammer, the focus of the film and book *The King's Speech*.

Having seen in the Telegraph my take on the story of the King's psychic – the story of Dr Cannon and King Edward VIII – the man had telephoned me that week in December 2006. He shared with me his own take on that story.

Throughout his childhood, he had been repeatedly told stories about Dr Cannon and the King by his father, a man called Piers Compton. Blaise Compton had got in touch with me because he wanted to explain the full story about the occultist guru 'His Excellency' Sir Dr Cannon and his clinic; what his Black Shirt father and his very wealthy fascist friends knew about Dr Cannon; and how secret agents were sent in to Dr Cannon's clinic just before the abdication of Edward VIII. Not only all of that, but most crucially of all, a top secret wartime raid on the Arctic Lofoten Islands had been conducted "under Dr Cannon's occult supervision".

Blaise Compton, the man on the end of the telephone, promised to send me a cassette tape recording of two men which he had made in 1985. Both men – Piers Compton and John Gastor – were dead soon after, one of them murdered. But, he said, listen to the story, listen closely to the recording as they tell it: "I never believed it until I saw your story, Mr Stowell. Now it seems to hang together so well." Dots had been joined, gaps in stories cleared up.

7

On that hangover Saturday in December 2006, the doorbell rang. I felt a rush of excitement. It was indeed the postman. He did have a package to give me. It was Odessa Day.

There was no cassette tape player in the kitchen – the only one within easy reach, luckily for me, was in our ancient car in the garage where it was quiet. Leaving my kids giggling around the kitchen table, I ripped the package open and escaped outdoors into the unseasonal outdoor warmth, got into the car put the cassette into the player, eventually running the battery almost flat.

Staring through the windscreen at a tangle of broken bikes, I listened to the voices of two posh, lively old men: one speaking for about 20 minutes, the other for 15.

Until that day, I thought I had the Cannon story to an extent nailed. I did not recognise the events or people being described on the tape. How to verify their claims? I felt overwhelmed. It would be hackneyed to say I was listening to a significant slice of secret history "revealed from beyond the grave" in my grotty old garage. But if what the two old men were saying back in 1985 was right, such journalese was certainly appropriate.

8

Of course I had known for some time how efficiently Cannon's name had been kept out of all versions of British history during the 1930s and '40s. But now the time had come to broaden my research. Gradually files of information and obscure out of print books piled up, allowing me to begin to join dots to create a picture of this doctor who was in equal measure intelligent, contradictory, deeply eccentric, self promoting and secretive.

Cannon's published work is still referred to by some practising British hypnotists; he is also known as an 'occultist' to a select number of hippies and goths in places like Whitby and Cornwall. But when he was active in the 1930s and early '40s, only a handful of those in powerful positions in government knew what he was up to in the corridors of power in London's royal palaces and Whitehall. There were very good reasons to allow Dr Cannon to fool the world into thinking he was just an eccentric. So who *was* he? Was he just a compulsive liar? Did Churchill know about what he was up to? Where did he come from?

Alexander Cannon's birth was registered in Leeds in August 1896, although another document puts his date of birth as a year earlier (he always loved to keep people guessing). Most of Leeds at that time was a vibrant, stinky place: street after street of atrocious slums, factories and mill sweatshops. Showering soot made it a city of endless front step scrubbing and net curtain washing for the women. Coal mines and ironworks on the outskirts provided badly-paid employment and life-threatening lung conditions for the men. But 'where there's muck there's brass', and the combination of mineral wealth, water power and Yorkshire grit had already made it the banking capital of the county. By coincidence, the city was briefly home to a man who played a major role in Cannon's story.

9

The future Archbishop of Canterbury, Dr Cosmo Lang, had arrived in Leeds in the autumn of 1890, to work as a priest at Leeds Parish Church in a district known as Kirkgate, one of the poorest areas of the city where he noted that many of the women were alleged to be prostitutes. It was, he said, "...the most squalid part of Leeds... I never saw anything worse, or even as bad, in East London."

A high-minded churchman, Lang perhaps hadn't noticed that close to the Parish Church, in 1888, a French engineer, Monsieur

Louis Le Prince, had filmed what were the first moving pictures using a single lens camera. And he would certainly never have visited the Leeds City Varieties whose stage was made famous in the BBC's *Good old Days,* a stage on which Cannon and his friend Salamander would have happily performed the sealed-in-the-coffin 'Message from Beyond' routine, along with the Indian rope trick.

While Lang noticed squalor, the boy Cannon years later became a product of the city's inventiveness and money-making traits. You could imagine his greatest influence was Heath Robinson, creator of fantastical machines: in the early 1930s, Cannon 'invented' the 'psychostehokyrtographymanometer' – which he said measured whether a couple was in love – along with the lie detector, a 'black light machine' and a number of eccentric electrical implements designed to ease the stress of mental illness.

Strange it was that Lang started out in his career in Cannon's place of birth, and that the doctor would end up representing 'Black Magic' which the archbishop believed threatened the monarchy. In a roundabout way, Cannon would be – briefly – extremely important to Lang, helping him intentionally or otherwise to change the course of England's history.

10

The influence of trips to the City Varieties as a boy stayed with Cannon: his speaking style reflected that of the music hall master of ceremonies. Not only did he love the sound of his own voice, but he also chose to wear every day of his adult life the suits, the spats and collars of a Victorian gent. No surprise therefore that he spent his last years entertaining audiences as a stage magician.

A much stronger, defining, influence in his life was his father. The family ended up taking over a hotel in the east coast resort of Bridlington. There, lay missionary James Cannon found willing ears to listen to his preaching, while his wife Marie welcomed a more regular income from her paying guests than the few coins her husband used to gather in the collection tins after mission meetings in Leeds.

Packed teatime prayer meetings on Bridlington's famous sandy beaches were an ideal venue for James to invoke the devil in the demon drink, the rights and wrongs and follies of the people, the wrath of God, and the dangers of the flesh. Cannon acquired a detailed knowledge of the Bible and repackaged it with music hall delivery. Indeed, in many of his ramblings about life, in his lectures, in his writings, if he was not directly quoting from the Bible, he presented whatever he was saying with biblical language ('And so it came to pass...'; 'For so it was that ...').

Another defining influence on him was the major trauma in his life – the First World War. The City of Leeds absent voters list of 1918 shows that an Alexander Cannon served with the Royal Army Medical Corps. The fact that Cannon entered medical school just a few months after the end of the war suggests that his interest in medicine had been stimulated by his experiences of the horrors of that war.

For his first year at Leeds University, he is listed under the First MB ChB in the printed lists of students. His subjects are physics, chemistry, zoology and botany, and his clinical on-the-job training was carried out at Leeds General Infirmary. He was active on the Medical Students' Council from 1920 to 1922, and he graduated in 1924 and later in 1928 as a fully qualified doctor.

He was registered with the General Medical Council in 1924, and then, rather unusually for his time, he went to study in China. Cannon researched his thesis subject – beri-beri – in Hong Kong, and his research was published in the British Medical Journal. A high achiever of considerable note, he asked for his degree to be awarded in absentia, with a supplementary report to be taken into account "owing to its great importance". He also advised that "from time to time I shall inform you of any further progress that is made in this most important disease of the East and Far East".

It was exactly when Cannon was doing his research that new treatments for beri-beri were being trialed. This crippling, often fatal, muscle-wasting disease is caused by a lack of the vitamin B strain of thiamine. It was prevalent in south east Asia, where polished white rice, which had lost its vitamin rich bran covering, was a staple food. Its prevalence was much reduced when the thiamine-rich covering was introduced back into the diet.

It is clear from his letter to the university that Cannon was heavily involved at that point in medical research into tropical diseases – there are references to his close contact with the Pasteur Institute in Saigon. But he relatively quickly turned his back on that research career line and began to explore a totally different area: oriental mysticism. He was in China and travelling around the Far East, where he could easily develop his mystic interests. Before that, he had been studying psychiatry in Vienna. It was an area of medicine which was undergoing a radical rethink in the wake of the massive toll of mental stress caused by the First World War.

So, in the late 1920s, Dr Cannon's career brought together two areas of great interest in the late 1920s and early 1930s, both of which were rooted in the First World War. Firstly, psychiatry had to adapt to the demands of dealing with millions of shell-shocked, deeply traumatized men. Secondly, millions of families left grieving for loved ones were creating demand for spiritualism and mysticism – and contact with the spirits of their dead menfolk. Dr Cannon was only too willing to lend a healing hand.

11

It might be a little controversial to say this, but some of the psychiatrists I have met are funny buggers. Cannon would fall into that category, and like most of them, he was a control freak too. But he was also a larger than life character who engendered great loyalty in his followers. They liked him for his apparently caring ways, and for the fact that he was developing new thinking. These were radical times, and his was definitely 'radical' thinking, some in the most extreme form.

Dr Cannon was definitely looking at alternatives to what was then the traditional approach to psychiatry: huge asylums where all 'deviants' – the mentally ill, unmarried mothers, the physically disabled and people with learning difficulties – were gathered up and locked away. The aim of psychiatry had very little to do with curative therapy, more to do with total control and isolation. It was the dreadful psychological impact of the First World War which brought changes, and Dr Cannon was helping them along, albeit in a bizarre way.

The world's most famous psychiatrist Sigmund Freud claimed that his 'therapeutic arsenal contains only two weapons, electrotherapy and hypnotism.' Electrotherapy is a way of re-booting the human brain, like restarting a computer to deal with a processing error. It appeared to work, and psychiatrists used it, particularly to 'reboot' the dysfunctional minds of soldiers suffering the effects of trench warfare. Accidental fatal electrocutions were not uncommon.

Many cutting-edge developments in psychiatry – which Dr Cannon will have studied in the 1920s – stemmed straight out of those trenches, and many came out of Germany and Austria too. One of the most respected neurologists of his time was Max Nonne. Based in Hamburg, he treated 1,600 traumatised patients, some with hypnosis, achieving a status which Dr Cannon would have given his eye teeth for: he was said by followers to be 'Ein Zauberheiler', a magic healer.

Nonne began his career in hypnosis by treating a soldier who had been struck dumb by the terror of Flanders at the very beginning of the First World War. He took the view that the soldier's problems were psychological, not physical, and attempted hypnosis. Psychiatrists and neurologists were clamouring to discover the secret of his apparent success.

Nonne won far more publicity than Cannon ever did when he was asked to treat Bolshevik leader Vladimir Lenin. Like Cannon, he had the instinct of a born showman and his popular presentations were said to be 'part academic, part clinical lecture and part pure theatre'. As a student, Cannon will have come across the work of Nonne and other German therapists. One therapy for the treatment of soldiers struck dumb by their trauma was hopefully short-lived: a one centimetre steel ball was pushed forcefully into the back of the throat, and at the point of suffocation, the patient shrieked, which was taken as evidence he had rediscovered his voice.

But a treatment which really caught Cannon's eye was based on the delivery of low-voltage electric currents. It was pioneered by the

27

German psychiatrist Fritz Kaufmann, and it was one which chimed with Cannon's belief that electricity stimulated psychic parts of the human brain.

But Kaufmann had no interest in such things. He combined strict military discipline with his electrotherapies, like a battle of wills between himself and the patient. There was no escape. Kaufmann barked commands like a sergeant major whilst administering electric shocks to the affected part of the body, such as a soldier's paralysed leg, demanding that the soldier must overcome his disability.

Wards filled with soldiers suffering post-traumatic stress and needing rehabilitation were faced with individual doctors adapting the Kaufmann approach and delivering ever more painful and prolonged shocks while barking ever more brutal orders to shake the soldiers out of their original trauma.

12

Meanwhile, over the border in France a pharmacist named Émile Coué had noticed, in the post-war turmoil, that when he dispensed a placebo with an enthusiastic recommendation to his troubled customers, their condition sometimes improved. There can be no doubt that Cannon studied Coué's first book, published in 1920: *Self Mastery Through Autosuggestion*. His mantra was 'Every day in every way I'm getting better and better'. It was hailed as a marvellous system and sold like hot cakes, particularly in translation in America, where there was a great interest in 'practical psychology' – the idea being that since 90% of the mind is unused, there is lots of space left for 'self mastery'.

The unqualified Coué produced no academic papers, concentrating instead on writing articles for 'ordinary' people in magazines and newspaper articles about self hypnosis: the blocking of harmful suggestions from others and promotion of healthy choices.

When he visited England in the early '20s, he ran séances at Eton School. His enthusiastic followers included the Governor of the Bank of England; Mrs. Vandebilt; Lord Curzon; the King of Belgium and the wife of Admiral Lord Beatty – an American heiress who suffered from depression. Looking like the K.F.C. Colonel, Coué mingled with his audiences after a séance or talk, and managed to get Lady Beatty to use her influence to have him invited to Tooting Special Neurological Hospital, where victims of shell shock were treated. Dr Cannon came into contact with some of these very people in his work some years later.

When Monsieur Coué was making a sensational visit to New York in 1923, Cannon was in Hong Kong, researching beri-beri. He would have read the ecstatic headlines from New York about Coué's arrival on Broadway, with Fred Astaire singing his 'better and better' mantra set to music by Jerome and Schwarz, and newspapers serializing *Self Mastery Through Conscious Autosuggestion*. The Americans loved this modest man with his accentuation on the positive; they were thrilled that Henry Ford trumpeted the benefits of Coué's ideas, and impressed that any money Coué made from his books and appearances was invested in his own foundation in Nancy in France.

Coué's death in 1926, aged 69, left the door wide open for a well-informed doctor and showman like Cannon to step in and steal his ideas. Back in England in 1930 Cannon began just that process, changing into Cannon the mystic hypnotist therapist, tapping into the lucrative market created by Monsieur Coué of well-to-do patients in search of cures from anything from nervous problems to addictive drinking.

13

When Cannon arrived to study in Vienna, the city's most famous son, Sigmund Freud, was developing what he is best known for: psychoanalysis. Elements of psycho-therapeutic theories can be found in Dr Cannon's books. His studies in the Vienna of the 1920s coincided with the work of other students and professionals such as Carl Jung, Alfred Alder and Erich Fromm, who were endlessly discussing, adapting and adding to the theory, an exciting process for any student to witness from the sidelines. Cannon made academic friends in Vienna whom he quoted throughout his life.

But Cannon was also attracted by the city's unique concentration of aristocrats, like the Rothschilds, with their glamorous palaces and their own fascination with mysticism. Vienna was the fashionable place to be in the 1920s, and it was here that the young Prince of Wales (later Edward VIII) was said to have received in secret one of his first bouts of therapy for addictive drinking from Dr Cannon, who was said to be 'the leader of a group of radical osteopaths' offering such treatments.

It was an early taste of what Cannon encapsulated – a Yorkshire childhood steeped in Christianity; his experience of some of the horrors of the First World War; an exacting medical training, followed by adventures with radical new thinking. Cannon was beginning the process of crafting himself into a powerful figure.

But there was one person who could derail his success: his wife, Eileen.

14

In every fold black sheep abound, and even in the Yoga Philosophy, occasionally there are those saints who fall away from their high ideals and begin to use their developed powers for selfish ends.

Alexander Cannon
The Invisible Influence
1933

Given the story of Cannon's short marriage, it is understandable that, from 1932 onwards, he absolutely denied the existence of a wife and daughter. The records of his divorce proceedings have lain untouched in a file in London for more than 80 years.

Alexander and Eileen Cannon had begun married life in Nanning in southern China and then moved to Canton, where Cannon worked as a prison doctor. Canton was on the 'Silk Road', an ancient trading route that linked southern China with India and south east Asia. They lived in the up-market Shameen district, an interesting and vibrant place, a European colonial settlement within China built on a small artificial island in the centre of Canton where it would be possible to live a fantastic high life on Cannon's salary. Shameen is 1250 yards long and 450 yards wide but full of markets, herbs and spices, fabrics from across Asia, rich with history, culture and religion: a great stimulus to Cannon's fascination with Eastern medicine. Elegant colonial-style buildings are still to be found there with newly married couples posing for wedding photos in the picturesque settings. No such romance blossomed for the Cannons however.

15

The brutal regime within Victoria Prison had hardly changed since it was built in 1841 and prisoners were kept in cramped shared cells. A variety of punishments were used by the English authorities as Hong Kong developed into a thriving port in the twentieth century. The perception was that criminals coming from the Chinese 'mainland' had to be 'flogged, branded and banished by transportation off Hong Kong Island' to keep crime levels under control. According to recent research, the abandonment of flogging was delayed until decades after the Second World War – it had widespread support amongst the Chinese and European communities as a tool of social and political control.

Back in Cannon's time, it is not hard to imagine what a dark place that prison was. He never recorded his reaction, although no doubt he had to deal with injuries caused by the beatings and floggings. And he was very well qualified to treat them effectively for the rampant beri-beri.

Cannon seemed to be well-established in his career. But something happened which meant he had to go back to England. Had he done something which would lower his reputation amongst his peers?

He returned to a lowly locum job on a salary of £30 at a hospital in Northampton. Cannon was nevertheless a highly successful medic who had not only studied at the Universities of Vienna and London, he had considerable medical experience in China and Hong Kong, and his research had been published. His wife Eileen, who had begun, and then abandoned, a degree in Leeds, was the daughter of a Church of England vicar from Dorset.

She began divorce proceedings as soon as they were back home. So what had happened between them? The question is particularly apt in the light of how rare divorce was back then, especially amongst the children of churchmen.

16

At county court in Bridport in Dorset on October 10th, 1932, Cannon faced serious accusations from his wife who had moved from Northampton and taken her daughter Wendy to live with her parents in Seaborough. Wendy at the time of the hearing was nearly four years old. She had been born in Hong Kong despite odds hugely stacked against her survival, on November 4th, 1928; before that, there had been a series of pregnancies which, Mrs Cannon claimed, her husband had terminated with forced injections.

The proceedings began with Eileen's evidence: "I was training at Leeds University when I met my husband. We went to live in China in Shameen in April 1926; we lived in Dr Reynold's house. Alexander got $600 or £70 a month. We could have had a servant but he did not want the expense, so I did all the cooking. When I asked for money he always asked if I could do with less. He is very mean. This got so difficult that I got a post as a teacher and even then he took money off me. He regarded me as his Chinese wife, to be submissive in every way. He is a very determined man.

"Taken in the round, my life has not been at all happy. Dr Cannon is an M.D. and a D.P.M. and has written books and pamphlets. He is a man of standing in the medical world. He borrowed money off my aunt when he had no need to. It was a lot of money. My husband had $25,000 in a fixed deposit account apart from what was in his current account when we returned to this country."

She implied that Cannon was brutal when it came to his favoured method of contraception. Mrs Cannon had already had a number of injections delivered by him when she began to suspect they were linked to her apparent failure to conceive, despite her husband's high sex drive.

"The manner in which he treated me was very lustful in nature. I did not find my husband at any time impotent. About the middle of June, I found a piece of foolscap paper on my dressing table. It was an account of a supposed fortune teller's visit. It was a prophecy that I was to have a child, which was not his, which would be born in July, dead. It was written in "Pidgin" English and it was in Dr Cannon's writing. I was very frightened. I asked my husband about it and he said he had written down what the fortune teller had said. He was always against having a family, saying it would injure my health to have a child.

"After this incident I was very upset. My husband said perhaps there was something in these fortune teller statements. He said 'Perhaps the best way would be to give you something to determine if you are in that condition or not.' It was then that he suggested further injections. I was very frightened. I have no doubt why the injections were given. He pressed with his wish to give me injections. I said that I had already consulted with my own doctor and that he should not do anything without consulting him. But I was reduced to such a frightened state that I allowed him to go ahead.

"It was at night. He put the case containing the ampules in the dressing table drawer. Next morning I took the case with me to see my own doctor. From what he told me I came to the conclusion that it was dangerous to me. I did not tell my husband of this visit to Dr Kirk. I would not allow any more injections because of what the doctor told me. Dr Kirk was very surprised I did not tell my husband when I thought I was pregnant…."

Mrs Cannon described how, during a ferry journey in China, she became sea sick. She had by then revealed to Cannon he was to become a father. Far from thrilled, Cannon gave her injections containing atropine, infundin and ernutin to get over her sea sickness: "The first injections were at Canton on the return journey by sea and I might have been in the earliest stages of pregnancy. He bullied me until I was forced to give consent. He raised his hand to me. He said the injections were to restore menstruation. On another occasion, I was about eight weeks advanced when I had a miscarriage. It was clear he did not want to have a baby."

When Eileen had again fallen pregnant and tried to hide the fact from Cannon, she described a car accident in which she was injured three months before she gave birth. She had been thrown out of the car by the impact. She was never sure if he had crashed on purpose to end the pregnancy. "My husband was also injured, but he took to his bed while I had to carry on as normal. The child was born on November 4th 1928. My husband gave me no money for my daughter's clothes. He gave me a child's bath, but that was sold back (to a doctor) when we left Hong Kong. Sometimes he was slightly affectionate but used strong language if our baby cried. His attitude was a matter of comment from friends. Frequently I protested especially about the tone of his language. In reply he would say I could either go and drown myself or find someone else who would treat me better.

"What I really fear is that I or my child would not be safe if I went back to him. I cannot trust him. I told him I am sick of living off and with my parents. It was unfair. When he said 'As you sow, so you shall reap', I took that to mean if I returned to him, things would be as bad as they were in Hong Kong. Then he sent me some money and from his subsequent letters I have felt some re-assurance is required of his behaviour. The thought of living under the same roof as him frightens me. When he came to Seaborough, I felt as though I could not receive him as I was afraid of what he might do. If driven to desperation, I feared he might resort to violence if I had gone back to the house in the asylum."

17

There certainly seemed to be a case for Cannon to answer. What is therefore all the more remarkable is Cannon's lack of reaction. Was she a neurotic fantasist, or a clever woman who, despite the times she lived in, finally stood up for herself? Was Cannon a psychopath, or a man in denial, the guilt building up to re-emerge in the future?

When Cannon responded to Eileen's allegations, it was with deadpan delivery: "I qualified as an M.B. in 1924 and an M.D. in 1928. I have held appointments in China as stated by my wife's evidence. I lived very happily with my wife in China. I hear what she said as to injections in Canton. I gave my wife no such injections. Neither did I hear of any miscarriage in Hong Kong until yesterday. I gave her no injections there either. I heard nothing of the last pregnancy until Dr Kirk congratulated me."

Eileen was granted her decree. For a few hours she had her revenge, but her moment in court was short-lived and made little or no impact. Had the same accusations been made and proven today, the police would have been called in and Cannon would have faced a prison term for coercing her to suffer painful and distressing home abortions. Yet he remained registered with the General Medical Council for the rest of his life.

18

Once Cannon had made his statement, he travelled back to Northampton General, no doubt glad that it was some distance from Bridport, and continued the process of building his brand as 'Dr Sir Alexander Cannon the mystic spiritualist healer and occultist'. He had learned very thoroughly one big lesson which he would never forget: always be in control. He was never going to be this vulnerable again. From the day the divorce was concluded, his wife and child did not exist. Cannon maintained that claim until he died: 'I have never been married, and never had any children.' Back then, there was no resort to the tabloids. Eileen kept her silence and everyone believed his story.

Brushing that court appearance under the carpet, Dr Cannon went back to his room in Northampton Hospital, pulled out his typewriter and carried on proof reading the book which would reveal his true greatness to the world, the book which would carry the title *The Invisible influence.* As a man thinketh in his heart, so will he be known: one of his father's favourite tenets.

Eileen's evidence must be ignored, he told himself, written out of existence; not worthy of him as a man of vision, a prophet, destined to leave his imprint on the sands of time. His opening paragraph was suitably grand:

'INFLUENCE! That word of nine letters carries a potency so terrible that kings reel off their thrones, armies stand aghast before its pitiful sound, electrified as it were into obedience…'

So what if Eileen had opened his bank account to scrutiny, called him mean, referred to his low pay as a locum job as a ward doctor – without seeing that it was evidence of his dedication to his profession. And she had always been resentful that her aunt had so believed in his powers that she lent him a large sum of money. He had come out of his marriage with $25,000 stashed away in his account to rebuild his identity and reputation.

True, he had to glance over his shoulder more often than he cared to admit, in case the General Medical Council came knocking on his door, asking questions about Eileen's 'lies'. But he could reassure himself that Northampton was a long way from Bridport. And Northampton was a place which could provide him with the perfect setting to make the right connections, build up a reputation as the 'master of black magic in England' and gain access through the most closely guarded doors in the realm.

Northampton was a sizeable town with a population of just under 100,000, nothing like his birth city of Leeds – no slums to speak of, and dominated by one industry: its shoes and boots were worn the world over. But by the 1930s, export markets had shrunk and the town was far from insulated from the effects of the depression, something the British Union of Fascists were able to exploit.

It was, and still is, the very heart of the Daily Mail's Middle England, a market town with an industrial base surrounded by quaint villages with squires, church spires and ancient histories. A well-respected local newspaper each week fostered a strong Northamptonian identity. Sixty miles from London, with regular trains to and from the city, the villages here were close enough to the capital to become over-spill playgrounds for the rich. The opening of an aerodrome at the village of Sywell in 1928 provided a stop-off for a newly-mobile brand of the cocktail set. An art-deco club house opened soon after for the comfort of thirsty passengers and pilots waiting for chauffeurs to drive them to their country house parties.

Five and a half miles due north of Northampton Hospital was one such playground: the village of Pitsford. Quaint it certainly is: Thimble Cottage, Wharf Cottage and Virginia Cottage grace the High Street; drive a little further on, take a right and then another right turn, and you will find a Georgian manor: Pitsford Hall, which is now a school. It has a tall, grand façade, and is set in 25 acres of ancient woodland.

Pitsford was another glamorous setting for another Cannon episode, this time another rebirth after his nemesis in the divorce court of Bridport. The man who made his rise and rise possible was Cannon's soon-to-be close friend, the Squire of Pitsford, Captain George Drummond, chairman of the London branch of Drummond's Bank, former High Sheriff of Northamptonshire, twice President of the Northampton Agricultural Society and President of Northamptonshire Cricket Club for five years.

When Drummond's Bank was founded in the eighteenth century, customers included Capability Brown, Josiah Wedgwood and Thomas Gainsborough. In the twentieth century, the Drummonds continued to be bankers to many of the rich and famous of their time, including Elizabeth Bowes Lyon and Lord Redesdale's daughter Diana, second wife of Sir Oswald Mosley.

After being disfigured by a severe injury to the top of his skull sustained during the Battle of Ypres in the First World War and a long period of recuperation, Captain Drummond bought Pitsford Hall in March 1919. It was the perfect location for him to start life with his young bride Kathleen, a Canadian who shared his passion for horses and hunting.

They also shared that passion with the royal family, and most notably with the dashing young Prince of Wales, the man destined to become King Edward VIII. Drummond was master of the famous Pytchley Hunt, and would lead the Prince and his brother Bertie out into the field. Bertie, the future King George VI, also brought his wife and two daughters Elizabeth and Margaret to stay at Pitsford where villagers smiled at their nanny when she took the princesses for walks. The small conservatory at the front of the house was added by Captain Drummond so that the then Queen Mother, Queen Mary, could observe her granddaughters taking riding lessons on the front lawn.

21

Village gossip has it that the dashing Edward enjoyed rather more than just the hunt and the lavish dinner parties which Drummond laid on at Pitsford. It was said he enjoyed the body of Kathleen a little too often and in fact fathered Edwina, the third of the Drummonds' four daughters.

One villager told a Sunday Times reporter in 1999: "We were always told not to stare at the royals. But we couldn't help it. Edward would come and sit in the Drummond pew (at church). No doubt about it. Edwina was his daughter. Everyone knew she was different from the others."

Villagers shared and relished the rumour that George had discovered his wife Kathleen in a compromising position with the then prince in the stable block. The Sunday Times story continued: "Drummond, a towering man, is said to have declared to the Prince: 'I will share my wine and horses with any man, but I will share my wife with no man!'"

A former local policeman told the newspaper that stories were passed down to him by his mother, who worked in service at the house, about the young girl who had a turned-up nose unlike the aquiline features of her three sisters, and was shorter than them, just like Edward: "Edwina was the prince's daughter. Everyone knew she was different. Her sisters were prepared to rough it and mix with the villagers. Edwina expected to be waited on. She was always the odd one out."

22

Kathleen died of pneumonia in 1933, and Drummond years later married a woman who became close to Cannon when both men moved to the Isle of Man. Honora Drummond was also quoted in the Sunday Times article about how Kathleen had enjoyed the parties at Pitsford: "My husband was strict and censorious. Kathleen was highly-strung and was the life and soul of the party. It was thus natural that when the party-going Prince arrived she would be attracted to him."

Also attracted to the Prince, but for different reasons, was another Pitsford regular, Dr Cannon. Whilst working on a relatively low wage at Northampton from 1930 to 1934, Cannon built up a stunning treasure trove of contacts in his address book by attending the Pitsford parties. He enthralled Drummond's wealthy friends with his Eastern mysticism and tales of the occult, developing his voice of authority and mystery, always changing out of his hospital white coat into his immaculate Victorian garb. Those contacts would eventually provide the regular income and status to allow him to leave the hospital and go it alone.

Meeting the Squire of Pitsford was a very lucky break for Cannon. Drummond was a larger than life character, very like Kazuo Ishiguro's character, Lord Darlington, in the novel *Remains of the Day*, a story of unrequited love between Miss Kenton, Darlington's housekeeper, and Stevens, the butler. As the tale of that relationship-that-never-was unfolds, Stevens describes the elaborate dinner parties at Darlington Hall in the 1930s in the build-up to the war where guests included German and British heads of state hoping to help both sides come to an 'understanding' to prevent war. The book and film, starring Anthony Hopkins and Emma Thompson, slowly reveals that while Darlington was a Nazi appeaser, he failed to grasp the Nazis' true intentions.

Similarly, Drummond did indeed hold lavish dinners for the rich and famous from London's cocktail set. Apparently, his guests occasionally changed into Nazi uniforms for special events. Guest lists read like a Who's Who of London society, and included one Joachim von Ribbentrop, Hitler's special envoy and later foreign minister, a man who would have appreciated Drummond's swimming pool directly behind the house where a Nazi-style eagle was designed into the tiling.

Drummond came with the royal seal of approval, vital for Ribbentrop, a former wine merchant turned diplomat. Ribbentrop had become Hitler's favourite foreign-policy adviser, a man well-travelled and able to speak foreign languages, who beguiled the German leader with shameless sycophancy, telling him exactly what he wanted to hear. Not only did Edward admire Hitler, he was appreciative of the German language and culture because of the royal family's strong German roots. Meetings at Pitsford Hall with the Prince of Wales in attendance would offer Ribbentrop a chance to convey back to Hitler the future King's positive impressions of Germany. All this was grist to the mill.

Herein lies the difference between Drummond, and Ishiguro's imagined Lord Darlington. While Darlington could be described as a little naïve, Drummond was a brash, outspoken and committed Nazi supporter and vehement anti-Semite. He was president of the Northampton branch of a pro-Nazi organisation called The Link, which was the most anti-semitic and pro-Nazi of the estimated 26 groups and organisations set up in the 1930s in an attempt to boost business and financial links, and 'greater understanding' of Germany, despite its murderous expansionist policies. Sir Barry Dolmville, the man who founded the organisation, described Drummond as "madly pro-German and anti-Jew".

Meanwhile, the Northampton branch of the British Union of Fascists was growing fast. Sir Oswald Mosley spoke on a couple of occasions at the town's Guildhall and Drummond bankrolled him, giving him considerable assistance. Northampton was the scene of some of the more notable outbursts of anti-semitism in England. One particular incident was reported in the Northampton Independent although there was no evidential connection with Drummond: a pig's head dripping with blood was hung above a door of the town's synagogue on Overstone Road.

Drummond was so steeped in Nazi politics that he made regular trips to Germany, and according to his chauffeur Jack Brooks, he met not only Hitler but also Reinhard Heydrich, who was to become in later years the architect of the industrial gassing of millions. Ribbentrop had every incentive to foster relationships with Drummond and his friends.

23

But Ribbentrop cast a much wider social net beyond Drummond, across what became known as 'The Two Hundred Families': the most aristocratic, and, he assumed, most influential people in Britain. His was a 'campaign for acceptance' directed at Britain, and Drummond and his friends were playing a small part in it, combined with an economic role. Stephen Dorril, author of *Blackshirt*, describes a 'wild money-making scheme' developed in 1936 which

– had it been triggered – would have made a massive loan of £50-100 million – billions in today's money – available to Hitler through Mosley's banking contacts.

Stephen Dorril writes: "When shown details of the (money lending) scheme, Diana (Oswald Mosley's wife) commented: 'George Drummond was involved.' ... Everyone was aware of Drummond's German connections through membership of Anglo-German friendship societies and visits to Germany."

Dr Cannon and Ribbentrop, circulating in the same social circles at the same moment in history, had very different aims. But where Ribbentrop failed to achieve his aim of using the aristocrats as a Trojan horse to change the course of Britain's foreign policy, Cannon succeeded in his own, much smaller scale, very personal aims of gaining access, and translating his socialising and lobbying into opportunities to influence. He was mixing with old Admiralty sea dogs who were Nazi sympathisers, and a future king. His success at inveigling his way into the upper echelons of the state must have been beyond his wildest dreams, and he began making lots of money. Enough for him to open 'rooms' in Harley Street, then in Welbeck Street.

He relied heavily on Captain Drummond, and the royals turned a blind eye to Drummond's deeply dodgy connections. They were prepared to be godparents to Drummond's many children. And when the Prince of Wales, or King Edward VIII as he became, needed discreet help, Drummond was only too willing to recommend the psychic services of his close friend.

Only a small number of people in Britain could match Drummond for contacts with the Nazi regime, the prominent role he played in The Link, and his attempts to bolster Hitler's influence in Britain. But he remained a free man. Many Nazi supporters were interned for being far less active than Drummond.

But he eventually got the hard word – something which triggered his departure from English shores. One of his friends recalls, in a privately published book, the moment the police, and probably MI5 officers, paid Drummond a visit in late 1939.

"I called at Pitsford Hall one day early in the war and found several detectives questioning the Captain. While I was there he gave me £1,000 in cash, saying: 'Look after my family if I go inside; and if you do I'll look after yours.'"

Drummond was given the choice of prison or self-exile in the Isle of Man. He sold Pitsford Hall to the Amalgamated Engineering Union keeping the farmland, and moved to the Isle of Man to begin a life in exile. It simply would not have been cricket to bang up the royal bank manager, even if he was a vehement anti-Semite and dedicated follower of Adolf Hitler. He was isolated instead on an island which had a security service in place to watch him.

In May 1940, he attempted to justify to a newspaper reporter exactly why he was leaving Pitsford: "I am afraid I cannot fit myself in any longer with life as it is now lived in the English community. I have sounded life at almost every point of the social scale.

"I have made a prolonged deep study of men and women in recent years. I have fought for what I honestly and consciously believe to be a better system of benefit to Britain, the Empire, Europe and the world as a whole. For all my pains I have gained nothing but criticism... I feel I can no longer live and move in such close proximity to the manifold aspects of British life... I am not running away – I shall merely carry on from a distance."

Dr Cannon was to follow him there at the start of the war, but for very different reasons.

24

Knowledge is power: therefore whosoever desireth wisdom, let him put himself into that condition in which he knoweth nothing, and read about The Invisible Influence – the Master of Destiny.

Alexander Cannon

There is something 'Flash Gordon' about Dr. Cannon, though with a biblical twist. You could see him in the black and white 1930s cinema original, casting bolts of lightning at 'forces of evil' alongside superhero Gordon. Combine Cannon's 'end is nigh' preacher delivery with the batwing-collared cloaks which Dr Cannon wore in real life, and you end up with a potential master and mentor for young Flash, an argumentative Yorkshire know-all to ward off Ming the Merciless and the Shark Men.

Cannon saw himself as mentor to the masses who were in the thick of economic and political upheavals of the 1930s. It had dawned on him that he would not make his fortune through psychiatry and mysticism alone. His new life goal became writing books to establish himself as a prophet and a healer of sorts, prescribing the tools of self-help and mad-cap science for the greater good. There was a market too for gramophone records of his hypnosis sessions and lectures. Whole chapters of his books were based on lectures he made in Bridlington, Mayfair in London, and in Bournemouth. His self-help hypnosis books and rambling records could feed off each other.

Whilst Cannon was a pioneer of sorts, the expression 'self-help' had in fact emerged over 70 years earlier as the title of a book *Self-*

Help by the Scottish author and government reformer Samuel Smiles. With chapters on "Money – Its Use and Abuse" and "Application and Perseverance", it sold 20,000 copies in 1859. By the time of Smiles's death five decades later, it had sold 250,000 copies, spawning an industry that traditionally has a big boost in January, when even readers who claim to detest the idea of transformation are tempted into buying life-altering guides.

Cannon was definitely on to a good thing. Self-help remains the biggest selling genre in the world, and Cannon was still amongst the first to commercially exploit the market. But as he unleashed himself into the publishing world, he had to simultaneously set about creating the foundation of the Cannon brand. He took great care in doing that over the mid-1930s in two stages. Stage one: be single-minded and totally focused on creating a new persona. Stage two: recruit his female mediums.

Once he had done that, he believed he was on course to become the self-help guru of the new media age as cracks appeared in religious faith. So Cannon entwined the biblical references with a smattering of Freud on conscious and subconscious functions and desires. He was a preacher-cum-psychologist who pointed to social, emotional and career problems arising from failure to discipline lusty groins.

The meaning of life was knitted into a strategy for mending your sinning ways, even though Freud's ideas were and are viewed as deeply non-Christian. If he had read his son's book, old preacher Mr Cannon Senior might have seen the devil take control of his son, and prescribed exorcism and perhaps a ducking at Bridlington Baths.

But Cannon had travelled beyond his influence, and as if to prove he was now on a higher social stratum, he dropped names into his text like sixpences in a Christmas pudding, like the 'very eminent' Sir Oliver Lodge, professor of physics at Liverpool University, friend of Conan Doyle; also one Walter Kilner, who Cannon described as a 'medical electrician'. He however attracted ridicule by extolling the special skills of Monsieur Moll, a French surgeon who specialised in hypnotising chickens, frogs, crayfish and guinea pigs, hoping for a cure for 'hysterical' patients.

Our spat-wearing master of wholesome goodness took readers of his books by the hand on a magic carpet tour of his own Far Eastern experiences and mixed them in with encounters with his rich and famous friends and clients, some referred to as 'Lord X' and 'Lady Y', to spare their blushes where appropriate.

In one instance, a 'lady of some standing' contacted Cannon as she suspected her husband was attracted to children – and she had been told a curse would fall on the child who was the subject of the attraction. (A strange little story, told through direct quotes from a letter which reads like it came straight from Cannon's imagination, and which concludes without any reference to the rather worrying suspicion of paedophilia.)

Like grown-up Harry Potters with more hang-ups than the Royal Academy galleries, readers of – and believers in – Cannon's new way of living found themselves hovering over stately homes peering into the parlours of his rich clients, with their sexual, drink and relationship issues. The themes of lust, inadequacy and envy emerge again and again.

25

When not preaching but discussing black magic, his texts are super ridiculous – how a 'famous' judge who was a friend of his (always very top drawer, never a 'manual worker') drove through a fierce fire around a bridge and the occupants of his car felt cold as he did so. Later they discovered a black magician had cast a spell on the bridge, the hero judge – in touch with his mystical side – had protected them.

In the 1930s, Cannon carefully crafted his appeal to anyone vulnerable, gullible or people who were keen to restore 'the way things used to be' as a reaction against industrialisation and materialism. Back then, there was a far greater appetite for a return to rural mysticism; there was tolerance of self-appointed prophets pontificating about the mysteries of life and the world, making up their own versions of science and history. Like most prophets, Cannon was right at the centre of his own universe.

He drew on his past experiences; he was listening carefully to those around him. Especially to those who were inventing their own versions of history and mythology, such as the far right. Once published, there was a surprisingly broad spectrum of influential people following him.

26

There was official interest in the West in brainwashing techniques before, during and after the war. Such methods were in fact used by some British interrogators, according to evidence unearthed by the BBC. They included drugs, hypnosis and sensory deprivation to extract confessions from suspected spies. There is internet chatter that Dr Cannon was involved in developing these techniques, which would make sense given his specialisms.

He certainly wrote enough to attract interest from those in dark recesses of Whitehall assessing the dark arts: "The Aryan Hindoos devoted centuries to unravelling the secrets of controlling the human mind… Their philosophy was one of deeds not words... they understood that 'impossible' was the adjective of fools; fear is proof of a degenerate mind... one must be master of his own faculties and slave to none of his desires..."

Such language would set pulses racing in those looking for the 'dawn of a New Order', or for control over unruly masses at home – or in the colonies. For excitable folk like the banker to the royals, Captain George Drummond, Cannon's words will have worked their magic and at least guaranteed the doctor an introduction to a wider and equally excitable, goose-stepping circle, especially when it came to the pro-German Edward and aristocrats worried about the demise of the British Empire.

Whilst not an obvious Nazi sympathizer, Dr Cannon nevertheless drew on Nazi mythology around the Aryan race in his writings, and more specifically the 'Aryan Hindoos' (sic). Thousands of years ago, so went his lunatic theory, they had created a whole civilisation when Britons were still savages: "Aryan Hindoo Masters held all the secrets ever discovered by man with regard to the mind control over another." Complete madness, but powerful words in the context of the 1930s.

Cannon takes things a few steps further: "The Aryan adepts (highly-trained experts) now, as of old, first hypnotize themselves and whilst in that state communicate with their subjects' unconscious mind by telepathy and so cause any hallucination, illusion or delusion they see fit to suggest. They are very powerful and their work extends from north to south, east to west... they are indeed masters of the mind of man..."

This *Manchurian Candidate* -style scenario was ridiculous then as now. Cannon was connecting political myths around 'Aryans' with the power of the occult in the minds of his readers. But there were those in government who were into aspects of this stuff, or at least were curious about it. One or two say Churchill most definitely was.

28

Cannon had completed the invention of his own chaotic 'brand' when Rider Books, the most established and well respected publishers of occult writers, and Charles Brendon of The Mayflower Press, a keen huntsman like Drummond, took a gamble on him, and he signed up with them. They too had perceived the growing interest in mysticism, and they had also spotted the market in self-help therapy books too.

Cannon, along with Émile Coué, was joining the ranks of pioneers of the self-help book; he wanted to nurture a reputation for helping people out of a mental rut, offering new thoughts, new visions, and hence new ambitions – exactly the mission statement of a book which came out a few years after Cannon's best-sellers, but which itself became a far greater and global success: *How to Win Friends and Influence People*, published in 1936 by Dale Carnegie.

Dr Cannon was a spiritualist, at his core were beliefs that the spirit "transcends the death of a body and that mediums can act as conduits between the physical world and the spirit world". The shared principles of present day spiritualists are no different from the beliefs held in the 1930s: that there is an infinite and all-governing intelligence; that individual identity survives death; that the spirit continues to learn after death; that communion exists between the physical and the spiritual realms; and that everyone is responsible for how to live out his or her life.

In the years immediately after the First World War and then into the 1930s, there were millions of broken hearts and broken ties of friendship and love. The survivors wanted to contact loved ones and deal with their grief – and like armies of spiritualists, Cannon was there to help them.

29

In his ramblings, he loved nothing more than to blur the lines between religious preaching and science. Take, for instance, the power of tuning into 'vibrating minds', a skill he claimed throughout his career, a particular noteworthy brain being that of Adolf Hitler, allowing him access to his military plans.

In *The Powers That Be*, written well before the war, he expounded the theory of negative versus good vibrations "...just like Enrico Caruso could shatter a glass with his vibrating voice, so too vibrating negative thoughts impact on the body. You must understand that you live in a world of spiritual forces that are operating all around you, for you are like one of those wireless-controlled battleships, guided by unseen forces."

Cannon had caught the eye of the rich and famous, and people in government, alarmed by those 'unseen forces' which were in reality social and political unrest. Anything was possible in World of Cannon, and science could be deployed to achieve whatever they wanted, even social control.

30

Back in the early days, he asked his readers, as opposed to patients, to buy into a moral code of abstemious, alcohol and tobacco-free living. "Perseverance, if it is not exercised, will atrophy... Daily exercise is essential to overcome obstacles. Nervousness, fear, brooding and doubt have to be vanquished."

But as well as evangelising an individualistic moral code in his book *The Powers That Be,* Cannon threw in a few extras above and beyond the self-help aspects. Persevere, and you, the reader, might become a faith healer in your own right, or an expert in hypnotism.

Chapter one   –   Oriental Hypnotism;
Chapter two   –   How To Get What You Want;
Chapter three   –   Telepathy – The Master of Destiny;
Chapter four   –   Faith Healing;
Chapter five   –   Black Magic –
                     the power of evil thought;

All leading to –
The Great Chapter – a study of the Mind, the Universe, Reincarnation, the Prophecies of the Bible, the Meaning of Numbers and the Book of Revelation.

His preface is written with the comic pomposity of an evangelist: "I confess I was, and still remain, a little dumbfounded by the miracle of the public response to my popular book, THE INVISIBLE INFLUENCE. (his capitals)

"(These miracles) came to me clothed in the familiar envelope; they came to me by telegram, telephone… from mechanistic and utilitarian (yet psychic) America…from business men and occultists, parsons and Indian colonels, doctors and judges, hard-headed lawyers, and women haunted by poltergeists.

"Faith has been unable to withstand the attacks of positive science, and so these people, becoming wavering and uncertain in their faith, have lost the support on which they depended and have been offered nothing of equal value to replace it. Science is above the heads of the ordinary mortal, and these facts probably help to explain the returning interest so many are evincing in magic and mysticism."

31

Mind telepathy was the first telegraph and telephone service on our Mother Earth

Alexander Cannon

Having spent some time exploring Dr Cannon's early years, I want you to lean back in your chair and relax every muscle in your body. Using the doctor's own metaphor, I want you to imagine those muscles are armies of workers. They need a break if they are to work effectively, so in your mind, go round your body and relax each and every one of them. Take a deep breath, and exhale slowly. Focus on your breathing.

Now imagine you are lying on your tummy on Dr Cannon's magic carpet, exhilarated, peering over the edge; you have a bird's eye view, flying through the clouds of time on your own. You are not cold. You are wildly excited.

It is 1932 and you are looking down on an urban landscape: the latest Morris cars, horse-drawn bread vans and coal lorries clattering along busy streets, smoke billowing from row after row of chimneys on row after row of terraced houses, creating a mass of grey cloud making you sneeze.

You are coming to the northern fringes of London: building site after building site, avenue after avenue of partly built art deco or mock tudor semi-detached houses: a vast, flat, bland suburban expanse.

Up ahead, on the horizon there is a building which seems to go on forever. It is low-rise, Italianate, with clock towers and cupola, set behind a dense wood. You hover and peer into an enormous free-standing corridor off which lead many other corridors which lead to four storeys of wards. You go higher and higher in the sky to take in the scale of the building. You are staggered. It is like a massive beast with a bony spine and rib cage: corridor after corridor, ward after ward. Hundreds of people call this home. All of them vulnerable to one maverick psychiatrist, one who has written so much about mind control.

32

Colney Hatch mental asylum first opened its doors in 1851. At the time of construction (on 199 acres bought from a local landowner), the asylum had 1250 beds and was the largest and most 'modern' asylum in Europe. At its height, it was home to 3500 mental health patients and had the longest corridor in Britain, the frontage was 1884 ft long. The building contained six miles of corridors, probably viewable from space like the Great Wall of China. It was once estimated that it would take a visitor more than five hours to walk the wards. For much of the 20th century, the asylum's name stirred fear and dread; it was not a hospital anyone would choose. 'Lunatics' stayed locked away for decades and most only left the building in a wooden box.

Colney Hatch had its own railway station, its own water supply, a chapel, cemetery and a 75 acre farm estate. The mentally ill could be kept efficiently hidden away without ever having to come into contact with the outside world.

In 1927, records show there were 494 nurses, 171 'probationers' and just nine full-time doctors. By 1932, one of them was Dr Cannon, still relatively young, trained, willing and able to hand out prescriptions and prescribe treatments. He had moved from Northampton where he had begun to build his private clientele. Here in London when he was not at work, he had much easier access to the rich and famous. The royal palaces were just down the road as were London's many paranormal societies who gathered to get in touch with dead relatives. And the day job at Colney Hatch provided a supply of patients from whom he could learn and on whom he could test his theories.

One can only wonder what he would have prescribed for the likes of the asylum's more notable patients, including Jack the Ripper suspect Aaron Kosminski, a man with a masturbatory disorder who starved himself to death; John Duffy, a serial rapist and murderer who had a double life, one as a respectable father of four, another a violent rapist stalking the streets for his next victim; and Dorothy Lawrence, a woman who was detained because she had dressed as a man to fight on the front lines in the First World War.

Perhaps he used a Freudian approach as a diagnostic framework, with hypnosis and electrotherapy as his tools, adding a few biblical lessons as reminders of the dangers of the flesh. Luckily for Dr Cannon's patients, lobotomies were yet to appear in the medical world – they were first carried out in America in 1936 and became more commonplace during the 1940s.

At Colney Hatch there were thousands of men, women and youths with a fascinating spectrum of mental illnesses, some simply social misfits, many completely and unjustifiably the wrong side of a cell door. But for the psychologist and psychiatrist with an interest in research and case studies, they were a veritable treasure trove of neuroses and illness. Dr Cannon must have thought he had died and gone to heaven – so many guinea pigs, so much scope to experiment.

33

Given the content of his books, some of his patients might have thought he was more in need of treatment than they were. But for the hospital managers, the stakes were high as long as he remained employed at the hospital with his books and theories becoming more publicly known.

It would not have taken much for a journalist to draw a comparison with the only other, and much more famous, occultist around at the time – 'The Great Beast 666' Aleister Crowley. What great potential for sensational headlines. Any reporter who picked up on such a story: *'Great Beast Rival Stalks Six Miles of Asylum Corridors'* would have been his news editor's dream.

And by a twist of fate, the two rivals were indeed to come face to face at Colney Hatch. Both were investigators and proponents of the occult; both believed in the power of 'the forces of evil'; both believed in reincarnation and in an infinite ability to expand the power of the human mind. But it was in Cannon's interest to emphasise their differences in order to protect himself and his reputation. He was determined to create the persona of a trustworthy mystic.

Where Cannon was 'respectable' in a non-conventional way, Crowley was a legendary bad boy, happily promoting his reputation as an upper class bisexual of independent means, famous for writing about gay sex – which was published abroad, for fear of prosecution; well-known for proclaiming the virtues of pure 'evil', and for his membership of some deeply weird secret societies. He was the media's ultimate bête noire and he relished their attention. Journalists dubbed him 'The Wickedest Man Alive'. Such is his cult, or occult, status, Ozzy Osbourne wrote a song about him ('Mr Crowley') and he is featured on the Beatles' Sergeant Pepper's album cover.

Both Crowley and Cannon were very much shaped by their deeply religious fathers. For Cannon, religion was a positive force, a tool to use in his treatment of patients; for Crowley, religion reminded him of the sadness and cruelty during his childhood, and he emphasised this in his writing and occult activities.

Whereas Crowley had achieved notoriety by the early 1930s and was known amongst the general public, Cannon was less well-known and, as a practising doctor, had more to lose by any association with The Beast.

In 1932, Crowley's second wife, Nicaraguan-born Maria Teresa Ferrari de Miramar, was admitted to Colney Hatch with alcohol and mental health problems. His first wife, Rose Kelly, had also been committed to an asylum with alcoholic dementia. Clearly marriage to Crowley was hazardous.

Suffering from delusions that she was the daughter of the King and Queen (Crowley and Cannon both claimed to be reincarnations of King Henry VIII), Maria came under the care of Dr Cannon.

Cannon at Colney Hatch was first and foremost a hospital doctor while pushing an alternative lifestyle. Crowley wrote in his diary: "Cannon has rather a bug in his brain over hypnosis. He advised me to leave Maria severely alone. He agreed that the case is hopeless, even should sanity temporarily return."

When visiting at Colney Hatch, Crowley was – rather amazingly – to test one of Dr Cannon's inventions – the psychograph – a device Dr Cannon had cobbled together to scientifically prove that telepathy was possible by tracing the breathing of two people, one of whom was sending a thought to the other. Changes in their breathing (tracked by a crude pressure gauge mechanism attached to the mouth, with the changes recorded in tracer graphs on rolls of paper) were meant to point to functioning telepathy when the two patterns matched.

Crowley had claimed to know "the secrets of yoga breathing", though when it came to using the psychograph to trace his own breathing, Crowley came a sad cropper as his wild lifestyle and unhealthy body meant that he could not breathe sufficiently deeply to enable the machine to work. One onlooker recalled: "Crowley, an exotic bon viveur with an incurable taste for ether cocktails… gave a deplorable performance."

The two men's paths crossed again more explosively one afternoon in May 1934. Cannon was delivering a lecture in a Mayfair hotel about the contents of one of his publications, his usual performances – yoga, levitation, Eastern philosophies – but more specifically about hypnotism. During the course of the performance, Cannon was hoping to hypnotise a young woman as a prelude to levitating her.

In Crowley's memoirs, he gleefully reported that Cannon blamed his failure to levitate her on the weight of her clothes: "Cannon said the experiment would have succeeded had it been possible to strip the girl naked in the main foyer of the hotel". Crowley was able to rib Cannon. One dry wit in the audience remarked that no-one would object to failure if a naked girl's body was available to admire.

35

Dr Cannon was attracting attention, but it was the wrong sort. He was starting to get coverage in the newspapers, and the Crowley encounter was reported in some back-page columns. This was brought to the attention of the hospital management and they had to take action. When Dr Cannon's first successful book, *The Invisible Influence*, hit the shelves, the hospital managers decided to sack him for conduct unbecoming for a hospital doctor – publishing a book about black magic, telepathy and hypnotism.

Dr Cannon took nothing lying down, so he immediately engaged a top flight lawyer to fight for his reinstatement. And the ensuing court battle, in which he conducted his own defence, attracted national and international headlines.

Clearly any psychiatrist claiming the reality of levitation was in need of attention from his colleagues. Amazingly, the courts agreed with Dr Cannon's defence and he did indeed win his job back. But at that moment, Dr Cannon was at a crucial stage in the development of the Cannon brand. He had to weigh up very carefully what he would do next.

36

The encounters with Crowley may have been bruising and probably contributed to his sacking, but Cannon was following his own advice and learning from his mistakes, taking the opportunity to build on what he had already created. He looked around at other masters of mystery, including popular stage acts of the time. Female assistants were employed to enhance the magic man at the centre of things. After all, Crowley had his 'Voodoo princess'.

His 'man of mystery' reputation needed extra embroidery. His mind drifted back to his childhood days at shows at the City Varieties in Leeds and in Bridlington, where stage magicians had enthralled him. He had copied their costumes with his batwing collars, cloaks and spats. What he needed was – a glamorous assistant to manage his life and look sexy. Cannon rather fancied making an assistant an integral part of the hypnotic treatments he was developing to help deliver the complete magical, mystical service.

Well versed in medical history, he looked back to the days of Louis XVI's court of the 1780s and the man said by some to be the father of hypnotism, or mesmerism, the Marquis de Puységur, who used a psychic assistant or medium. He would put her in a trance and ask her to glare at a patient and deliver a diagnosis of illness.

Like Dr Cannon, de Puységur was happy to be a black sheep of the scientific community. He experimented with, for example, extrasensory perception, exactly like Cannon himself. According to one writer, the Marquis became very famous and won support from some members of the government so that by the autumn of 1784, he was 'mesmerizing' on a huge scale with the enthusiastic support of local officials in his home town of Bayonne. Stories of his feats and records of cures he allegedly achieved by hypnosis spread like wildfire. If the Marquis de Puységur could do it back in 1784 with the help of a mediumistic assistant, so too would Dr Cannon.

37

Dr Cannon's ideal advert in the 'situations vacant' might have been as follows:

'Wanted: psychic woman, does not answer back, clever, will believe everything I tell her; should be ready to change her accent and name should it be required; able to cook and to generally look after my every need. In return: contact with posh people including royalty, own room, meals, and the opportunity to travel.'

That was exactly what he got. By a stroke of luck, when he found the ideal biddable girl, she had a beautiful teenage sister who he promptly also took under his wing. She in later years would become a useful attraction to the Cannon Clinic. For now though, he claimed the sisters were under his 'guardianship' – an assistant and a trainee.

The girls were from Sunderland, a working class town in the north east of England, probably vulnerable to a potential predator like Dr Cannon. He arranged for the girls to change their names and drilled them to change their accents. They proved to be a very good investment.

Nothing is known about the sisters' exact whereabouts when they first met Cannon except that he recruited Eleanor Diana Robson, the elder sister probably in 1935, Joyce a little later. Eleanor was a nurse in Harrogate, around 23 years old at the time, a plump girl with a kind face, rounded features and an eminently trustworthy and reliable nature; she looked well in her nurse's uniform, perfect in the role of official medium for Dr Cannon.

Their first séance or lecture was probably held at a hotel in Harrogate, a Yorkshire spa town not far from Leeds where hundreds of rich elderly people were preparing to make their journey to the Other Side, and willing and able to pay Dr Cannon to get in touch with relatives who had already made it.

Whilst Eleanor may not have been a crowd-puller – nor is there any evidence to suggest she described herself as psychic before they met – her sister certainly was, maturing into a dead ringer for Jane Fonda. She may have only been 17 years old when she came into the service of Cannon, but he certainly made the most of her attributes in the coming years. The names he chose were music hall style: Eleanor became 'Rhonda de Rhonda', and Joyce 'Joyce de Rhonda'. The titles 'Dames of St Hubert' were tagged on for good measure. When he changed the nurse uniforms for identical music hall style costumes, tongues began to wag, big time.

38

As Cannon got his act together, so too did the man who could be seen as his nemesis. An innately conservative churchman with a liberal streak, Dr Cosmo Gordon Lang, Archbishop of Canterbury throughout the 1930s, was alarmed that spiritualists and occultists like Dr Cannon were becoming more and more common; they seemed to be taking hold of many minds and fostering change. So he ordered an inquiry.

Dr Lang had become Britain's first celebrity archbishop, his life enmeshed with the royals in a way no other archbishop was or is ever likely to be. He had invented the 'royal walkabout' for George V and his Queen, and helped steer royal media coverage; he was a close friend and confidant of Queen Mary after she was widowed, and baptised Princess Elizabeth. He believed in tradition, and that the Church of England and the monarchy had to be preserved at all costs.

Very aware that he was living in a new media age, he was learning how to control events. He did what he thought was right at every turn. So, having instituted an inquiry into spiritualism, when the results were not to his liking, according to conspiracy theorists, he ensured that the final report remained under lock and key until well after his death.

Born in 1864 in Aberdeenshire, Lang was the son of a Scottish Presbyterian minister. As a young man he studied law at Oxford and was mixing with other students who were heading for ordination into the Church of England.

He was to follow them after he was gripped by "a masterful inward voice" which told him: "You are wanted. You are called. You must obey." He immediately gave up studying for the Bar, renounced his (Conservative) political ambitions and applied for a place at Cuddesdon College, a theological institution just outside Oxford. This decision disappointed his father, but he nevertheless wrote to his son: "What you think, prayerfully and solemnly, you ought to do – you must do – we will accept."

Ever obsessed by power and hierarchy, he quickly rose up C of E ranks and had played a prominent role in the 1911 coronation of King George V, getting closer to the royal family every day in every way, fawning at their feet. His famous love of the royals saw him described as "more courtier than cleric". He was Archbishop of Canterbury from 1928.

39

As time went on he could not hold back his instinct to help preserve the relationships between British institutions and the establishment, as well as those between government, the Church of England and his adored royal family; he could not help make apparent the fact that he was totally at odds with Edward, both as Prince of Wales and as king.

Always on hand to advise on public relations, Dr Lang was a clever tactician who kept an eye on what he saw as the public's well-being. A reluctant pragmatist, he eventually supported relaxing the divorce laws, supported a campaign against the death penalty and was instrumental in the Church giving its approval to some forms of contraception. When the divorce laws were eventually relaxed, he admitted it was no longer possible to "impose the full Christian standard by law on a largely non-Christian population".

His reaction to spiritualism was more circumspect and suspicious. Mystics like Dr Cannon claiming they could communicate with spirits had always been around, but now they were in the media, making money, becoming popular, and some were anti-Christian. Not only that, whilst it was OK for saints and holy men to claim to communicate with spirits, spiritualist salesmen like Dr Cannon advocated getting in touch with the dead from believers' front rooms.

Dr Lang decided to convene a panel of experts – academics, churchmen, psychologists – to assess exactly what was going on. One of the experts was Dr William Brown, an eminent Harley Street psychologist who would come across Lang and Cannon very personally and very directly during the abdication crisis.

The Committee studied the subject in great detail for two years and then handed in their findings. It was expected by the Committee and the concerned public that the guidance contained therein would be made available fairly quickly to the rank and file of the Church of England who, up to then, had been given no official lead regarding 'communication with the deceased'.

Lang and his bishops then decided by a large majority that the report should not be published. It was not until 1979 that the full text of the Majority Report was released and published in the journal 'The Christian Parapsychologist'.

The fact that the committee was convened and carried out an inquiry which was then hushed up may help tell its own story about Lang and his insecurities about the established church. If it was Dr Lang who ordered the report's shelving, it would be no surprise. He proved to be skilled at plotting – as Edward VIII and Dr Cannon were to find out.

40

To his clients or patients, Cannon was cutting edge, offering treatments no-one else did. He specialised in psychiatric approaches to addiction and other 'disorders of the mind' which many believed had only been tried in Vienna, where Dr Cannon had worked and studied. And it was there, so it was claimed by one of the apparently well-informed Blackshirts, that he first encountered Edward, Prince of Wales, in the late 1920s for 'a cure for addictive drinking'. Whether or not he did actually have a consultation back then, Edward appears to have been in Dr Cannon's mind at least when he wrote one of his books.

The Secret of Mind Power and How to Use It reads in one section like Dr Cannon was in a counselling session with Edward. He does not name him, but says he is describing someone carrying 'a great burden of destiny': "Let us forget for a moment the part we are playing on life's stage, and remove the mask we usually wear to disguise our true characters from ourselves and our fellow men.

"In doing this we shall become aware of many unfortunate habits and stumble upon desires which we would not dare disclose to our best friends.

"Turning one's back on one's work – or one's task in life – is the reaction called forth by the discord existing between one's personality and the demands of life."

Tommy Lascelles, one of Edward's aides during the 1920s and early 1930s, painted a picture of a drunken playboy prince with habits and flaws which made it difficult to deal with his 'great burden of destiny'. Lascelles, a cousin of the Earl of Harewood who had married Edward's sister Mary, not only saw Edward from a professional insider's view, but also got to hear jaundiced opinions from the rest of the royal family.

Having had such insight into royal dysfunction, Lascelles wrote the following text in 1943 on the strict understanding it was only for publication after Edward had died. It was recently published in the Daily Mail: "For some years after I joined his staff, in 1920, I had a great affection and admiration for the Prince of Wales. In the following eight years I saw him day in and day out.

"I saw him sober, and often as near drunk as doesn't matter; I travelled twice across Canada with him; I camped and tramped with him through Central Africa; in fact, I probably knew him as well as any man did. But, by 1927, my idol had feet – more than feet – of clay.

"Before the end of our Canadian trip that year, I felt in such despair about him that I told Stanley Baldwin (then Prime Minister, and one of our party in Canada) that the Heir Apparent, in his unbridled pursuit of wine and women, and of whatever selfish whim occupied him at the moment, was going rapidly to the devil and would soon become no fit wearer of the British Crown.

"I expected to get my head bitten off, but he agreed with every word. I went on: 'You know, sometimes when I am waiting to get the result of some point-to-point in which he is riding, I can't help thinking that the best thing that could happen to him, and to the country, would be for him to break his neck.'

"'God forgive me,' said Baldwin, 'I have often thought the same.' Then he undertook to have a straight talk with the Prince at an early opportunity; but he left it until October 1936 – too late, too late."

Lascelles wrote that at one point, Edward admitted to him: "I am quite the wrong person to be Prince of Wales."

42

Born on June 23 1894, Edward was often compared to Peter Pan. His upbringing was clearly dysfunctional. George V was a 'shy disciplinarian' with a famously bad temper, who found it difficult to communicate with his children. Edward knew his father viewed him as a failure.

Edward was tutored at home, went to naval college and Oxford, but did not mature while he was away from the glare of a disapproving father. He was bored by academic life and the rituals which his life encompassed as a royal; he never read books or disciplined himself to achieve anything other than his self-punishing exercise regime of running and starving himself – often thought to be a manifestation of self-loathing. The symptoms of anorexia nervosa were recognized in him as a child, to the extent that he may have been attempting to stave off puberty, so some authors claim.

As a 20-year-old, he was chasing excitement and thrills. In the First World War, he joined the Grenadier Guards despite only being five foot seven inches tall, of slight build and almost hairless – not the regulation six footer, nor much of a match for any Germans in the trenches. He was of course protected from danger, something else which troubled him, and became another source of resentment.

His sister Mary and brother Albert married in 1922 and 1923 to the delight of their parents while Edward continued to disappoint. Despite the playboy image, he sought mother figures in his women, and played at being a little boy lost, using baby language, changing certain words to make them sound 'cute'.

George V was enraged by Edward's failure to settle down, disgusted by his affairs with married women, and reluctant to see him inherit the Crown. "After I am dead," George said, "the boy will ruin himself in 12 months."

Like Dr Cannon, George V understood how Edward's "habits and desires", in Cannon's words, would lead him to "turn his back on his task in life" and lead him to pretending he was achieving what was expected of him by indulging in "drink or narcotics".

43

"What next?" Edward is reported to have resentfully complained when in January 1936, the day arrived for him to follow his father's coffin at the state funeral. By then he had already started his relationship with Mrs Simpson. Her impact on him in those early secretive months when the public knew nothing was noted by chaplains and other Church of England staff writing in diaries and journals held at Lambeth Palace, the headquarters of the Church of England.

The Chaplains pulled no punches, describing him as an arrogant, drunken spoilt child, judging him unable to complete his duties as Prince of Wales, and later as monarch, as he was fixated with Mrs

Simpson and could not function without her at his side. He had had relationships with a series of married women including textile heiress Freda Dudley Ward, and Lady Furness, the American wife of a British peer, who was the person who introduced the prince to her friend and fellow American, Wallis Simpson. The chaplains had had enough, and so too had the Archbishop.

Simpson had divorced her first husband in 1927. Her second husband, Ernest, was a British-American businessman. She and Edward became lovers while Lady Furness was out of the way, travelling abroad. Her existence weakened his relationship with his censorious and increasingly sickly father. His parents met Simpson once at Buckingham Palace in 1935, but refused to meet her again, and the King was dead by January 1936.

The Special Branch as well as Lambeth Palace got to hear of this scandalous relationship. An undated report detailed a visit by them to an antique shop, where the proprietor noted "that the lady seemed to have POW (Prince of Wales) completely under her thumb."

Anne Sebba, author of Mrs Simpson's biography *That Woman*, says Edward's need to be dominated and to adore did not please Mrs Simpson who found his devotion tiresome. His physical boy-like size led to an inadequate self-image, and, whilst his womanising was legendary, his female conquests referred to him as "the little man".

Anne Sebba writes: "He may have also worried that he was sterile. Without tests he is unlikely to have known whether or not this was the case, but heavy smoking and drinking are now known to have a drastic effect on sperm count, and he would have noticed that none of his dalliances (except that with Mrs. Drummond, allegedly) resulted in pregnancy.

"In the years since 1935, Wallis Simpson acquired the reputation of a seductress with legendary contractile vaginal talents. She had, according to one study 'the ability to make a matchstick feel like a cigar'."

To Sebba, MI6's China Dossier, which detailed what the Secret Services discovered about Mrs Simpson's bedroom skills whilst out in Shanghai as a younger woman, remains speculative by its very nature. Sebba refers to Wallis's world-renowned vaginal skills, her sexual appetite, her sexual domination of Edward and her habit of finding new ways to humiliate him in front of other people, all factors which, intentionally or otherwise, cemented him to her.

Royal biographer Philip Ziegler believed that Wallis provoked in him a slavish devotion, and profound sexual excitement, "possibly with sado-masochistic trimmings". To compound the torture for Edward in 1936 and even 1937, the year after his abdication, Mrs Simpson was writing love letters to the husband she was in the process of divorcing.

Historians claim had this been discovered at the time, it would have been a clear case of collusion and the King's Procter would have intervened and perhaps neither the divorce, nor the abdication would have taken place.

According to Anne Sebba, at one point, she actually told Ernest that she wanted to 'make an attempt to recapture her earlier life' and break with the King. She told him she had to return to the 'calm and congenial' life he offered her. Alone, Edward is said to have threatened suicide, swearing he would never let her go. If she tried to leave him, he said he would cut his throat; he even slept with a loaded pistol under his pillow.

In another letter to Ernest: "I wake up sometimes in the night and think I must be lying on that strange chaise longue and hear your footsteps coming down the passage of the flat and there you are with the Evening Standard under your arm! I can't believe that such a thing would have happened to two people who got along so well."

Sebba adds: "Privately, they continued to poke fun at the king, referring to him as the child that never grew up: Peter Pan... Wallis knew that, with less to play for, she behaved better with Ernest than with the King, and the security Ernest offered suddenly appeared as something to be cherished compared with the hate and loathing she increasingly had to face as the King's lover."

44

For decades, Edward's love of Mrs Simpson – and her love of him – was the official explanation of why the King abdicated. That has been blown apart in recent years.

It is understandable that in such a bizarre set of circumstances and personalities, Edward will have felt a great deal of pressure to 'man up'. Expectations could not have been higher. Turning to an unconventional and very secret guru for help will have had its attractions.

After the Second World War, John Gastor researched Dr Cannon's connections with Edward VIII and ended up with the following analysis: that Dr Cannon and Mrs Simpson were as much a 'sling around Edward's neck' as the other. His claim was that England's 'master of black magic' Dr Cannon was as much to blame for the abdication as Mrs Simpson. A fanciful assertion for sure, but it is one worth examining.

45

The cassette tape I listened to in December 2006 was for a long time the only source of the theory that Dr Cannon played a role, intentionally or otherwise, in Edward VIII's abdication, the result of a plot by Dr Lang to help him off the throne. Cannon was one of a number of ejector levers, not just the one 'Mrs Simpson' factor, as the official version had it. Edward's politics were another factor. A pity it took John Gastor almost 40 years to talk about what he knew. Even then, his Cannon story remains undisclosed until now.

Gastor's theory was that around any king there are 'king watchers' who control him – and also have the power to get rid of him. Dr Lang fitted into this category perfectly.

Hugely clever and well-connected, Gastor became an unpaid history researcher after the war when he sought out people deemed to be so dangerously pro-Nazi they were interned under article 18(b). Many of them were imprisoned on the Isle of Man in Peveril Camp, where they could pick up classified information because just like Gastor himself, some had connections within the secret service and government.

It was these fascist ex-detainees who, aside from lots of other things, happened to tell Gastor that King Edward was known to be seeing a mystic doctor in the run-up to abdication in 1936. This black magic dabbling they said, alongside Edward's pro-German stance, was 'the sling around the King's neck as deadly as Mrs Simpson'. So many people told him about Cannon – he was a man of enormous influence – and yet there was never a mention in the history books, not a word.

Gastor was a homosexual with far-right political leanings whose choice of research subjects alienated him from the rest of society. Some members of his own family could be found working closely with or for those in power; one or two worked for the British royal family. Hearing scandalous gossip about the rich and famous gave him an appetite for constructing his own versions of history. Gastor's brain was a vessel for history and rumour. He was a passionate debater, a good listener for sure, hanging on every word when a new nugget came his way to be either accepted or rejected. If he chose to reject, he was famous for exclaiming imperiously: "My man, you're a liar, you're simply a liar."

Aleister Crowley had numbered among Gastor's acquaintances along with many colourful characters snatched up from all over Europe in the whirlwind of the Second World War and deposited in London to rebuild their lives.

His research work had been unpaid, so to make ends meet, he got work as a messenger and reporter for an occult magazine, picking up copy from a wide range of writers all over London and returning it to the office for publication. That way he had mapped out the occult underworld. He witnessed séances and psychic experiments, including one mass event in the Albert Hall, another in the lounge of a house in Mayfair, another near the House of Commons. And he heard stories about Dr Cannon.

It was 1985 before Blaise Compton persuaded him to record his story onto a cassette tape – the year of Live Aid and Madonna's *Papa Don't Preach*. Gastor was feeling bewildered as the old certainties of the Cold War began to crumble. Wallis Simpson was still alive and Mikhail Gorbachev had become General Secretary of the Soviet Union, with Ronald Regan beginning his second term as US president. His diplomatic contacts had begun to talk of tiny glimmers of what was to become Glasnost. At home, the royal family was still to some extent revered by the British, but the tabloids had in many ways holed them below the line, or so it seemed. Prince Charles and his wife Diana had produced two sons, but their marriage was in trouble. Their every move was scrutinised. The avalanche of rumour, innuendo and gossip about the marriage included suggestions that Diana's wild spending had driven a henpecked Prince Charles to retreat into mysticism. The royal couple had given an unprecedented 45-minute television interview in an attempt to set the record straight. Gastor could see royal history beginning to repeat itself as far as troubled romance and mysticism were concerned.

Gastor talked at an incredible rate of knots once he got going, connecting people, historical facts and social trends to create his own version of things, often subverting official versions – punctuated with lots of "er's". His head and pockets were stuffed full of historical notelets and nuggets of classified information and sexual gossip, some dating back to the 1920s. A shame he didn't write it all down instead of relying on his disorganised filing cabinet of a brain.

When making the recording, Blaise Compton was relieved that at last he could sit and listen, although he did not know whether to believe what he was hearing. Gastor's considerable network of contacts were in the more desirable bars and clubs of London, though he himself lived in a squalid bedsit. He had recently upset a group of neo-Nazis by helping to expose a prominent charity which was a front organisation for their very nasty organisation.

"If the next time you visit me I am in a morgue, you will know what happened", he said to Blaise as he left.

And he was indeed murdered, bashed on the head in an attack on a London street. He died several days later in hospital, never having regained consciousness. No-one was ever prosecuted. It will never be known whether there was any connection with his helping to expose that far-right group.

46

Things are not how we're told they are.

Piers Compton, talking to his son on tape in 1985

Blaise had also persuaded his father, a far-right journalist and writer, to record his version of the 'Edward and Dr Cannon' story. He was delighted to finally get his father to record that story which he had heard so many times over the family dinner table when he was a boy in the 1950s: about the role in the abdication of a master of black magic; and how his father had one night, at the height of the abdication crisis, tracked down Dr Cannon to his clinic and confronted him.

Where John Gastor was a researcher, an outsider, Piers Compton was a Black Shirt foot soldier and supporter of British and European fascism throughout the 1930s and '40s. They were the only living people Blaise could find to confirm the Cannon story, and put more flesh on the royal bones.

Both men set out the likely reasons for Edward's secretly turning to Dr Cannon. They understood his psychological and personal problems and the rumours of the political forces working against his remaining on the throne

A far right intellectual and devout Catholic, Compton was a

supporter of the British Union of Fascists, or simply the British Union as it became known. Later in life, he spent thirteen years as the literary editor of the Catholic newspaper *The Universe;* in his early years he had been a priest. He never stopped writing historical books as well as newspaper pieces, tracing the evolution of the Catholic Church. He was also a ghost writer for eminent medical specialists.

Because of what he had learned about the plot to force Edward VIII to abdicate, conspiracy theories were never to be discounted without due consideration. When he was in his eighties he published *The Broken Cross*, in which he advanced the theory that the Vatican was infiltrated by the secret forces of the Illuminati and Satanism. Proof of those hidden forces came, according to Compton senior, when his book was immediately withdrawn from circulation on publication.

Blaise said: "My father would often take me to one side and say, 'Now look here – things are not how we are told they are'- and he would tell me the story of Cannon and the abdication – further proof of his theory. Events, so he said, were actually determined by other people and we are all acting as automatons. I reacted very strongly against these conspiracy theories."

Compton believed that "pro-war" forces in Britain, in the form of Prime Minister Stanley Baldwin, had used the existence of Cannon to get rid of "anti-war" King Edward, who wanted a rapprochement with Germany.

Growing up in a more optimistic and open post-war world in the 1960s, Blaise resented his father's repeated oppressive lectures at the dinner table. He questioned and then rejected his father's overall message that the world was dominated by secret forces. He felt deeply ambiguous about the story of Edward being secretly dominated by Cannon. Blaise said: "When he started telling me the Cannon story, it poisoned my life because it was a vindication of the conspiracy theory which I was trying to escape.

"He told me in detail about his encounter with Cannon at his clinic in London. He told me lots of detail about other stuff. Tales about, for example, Mrs. Simpson's esoteric tantric sexual skills picked up in a floating brothel in Shanghai. I was convinced they were examples of urban myths, that sort of thing, and that he had been completely taken in by them. But then I wondered how would he make up such stories from nothing?"

In the tape recording, Piers Compton tells the Cannon story in a very matter of fact way. He refers to characters active behind the scenes and, in one case, to an official only revealed as playing a part nearly twenty years later, in 2003. Even then, it was a few more years before the full extent of the conspiracy against Edward was realised.

Blaise said: "A number of years after my father died a book was published about the MI6 China dossier which went into the (alleged) detail of Mrs Simpson's soubriquet of "Shanghai Lil" – one of the stories I didn't want to believe. But there it was – in a book. Vindication, of sorts, at last, you could say."

47

An occultist hypnotist who practises dangerous methods of treatment

Archbishop Lang's description of Alexander Cannon

Further vindication of the Blackshirts' claims of a plot to get rid of Edward came unexpectedly three decades later with some neat detective work by a vicar from Essex, Dr Robert Beaken. He identified Lang's 'smoking gun' memo which exposes Dr Lang's plotting.

Further evidence is to be found in letters, diaries and memos I read back in 2006 which reveal the moment Dr Cannon popped up on Dr Lang's radar. Equally interestingly, some 'Plan B' plotting by Dr Lang revealed his intent to further exploit Dr Cannon's proximity to the king should he not have abdicated as fast as Lang wanted. But once Cannon and Edward's 'black magic' connection had been exposed to a very select few, Plan B was not required. But it serves to illustrate what was going on in Lang's mind, and how he might have planned to further exploit Cannon if necessary.

The Archbishop's radar mechanism was a 'gossipy network of chaplains and vicars' – the eyes and ears on the ground in his complex and powerful C of E institution. The Lambeth Palace archive shows that Cannon's moment of discovery triggered decisive communication and co-operation between Lang and Prime Minister Baldwin. At that point, the Downing Street – Lambeth Palace alliance became the noose around Edward's neck which the Blackshirts had described as tightening enough to make him abdicate.

48

The royal biographer Philip Ziegler says Archbishop Lang had from the start believed the King's proposal to marry a twice divorced woman and remain king was "simply inconceivable: a monstrosity". He had in any case decided there was no way Edward could remain on the throne. Lang would stop at nothing to ensure the survival of the two institutions – the monarchy and the Church of England – which he believed the English people held dear. They had to be protected from the threats of Edward's drunkenness and vulgar social circle.

Edward, who rarely went to church, was a million miles from Lang's expectations of a monarch and head of the Church of England. Then there were his speeches in support of Nazi Germany when he opposed intervening following Hitler's re-occupation of the Rhineland in March 1936; his flirting with fascism, his dismissive attitude to the old order, all reasons why he had to be replaced by his more stable brother George, who led a conventional family life.

Spinning more positively, author Dr. Susan Williams describes Edward's problems through Lang's eyes as "his modernity, his sense of democracy, his affected American accent, his visits to the poor." Unaffected by convention, Edward alarmed politicians by wading in with a comment that 'something should be done' about unemployment and poverty in South Wales following a highly-publicised visit.

Both embraced the new media age of the 1930s: Lang wanted to reinforce his own and the church's authority; Edward was keen to advertise his own good looks and boost his popularity. The English royals had only to look to the toppling monarchies in

Europe to realise they needed the support of the media in maintaining patronage and power. As access to radio and cinema slowly became universal, Lang had advised Edward's parents – George V and Queen Mary – to set a tradition of royal walkabouts. Edward's biographer Philip Ziegler describes Lang as devoted to the royal family in "an almost slavish way, believing that he in himself would provide a bond between church and monarchy which would sustain them both."

Edward himself picked up on that aspect of Lang, writing that he was "too close to statesmen and princes... more interested in prestige and power, a spectre clad in black moving noiselessly about". By the summer of 1936, Edward and Lang had been through embarrassing and bruising encounters attempting to plan ceremonial details for Edward's coronation. Edward was becoming alienated from the all-important religious establishment, failing to appreciate its power, especially as someone who enjoyed drinking and was unlikely to cement a suitable marriage with a young member of English nobility.

49

George V's death in January 1936 was a disaster for Lang as he knew that Edward would not continue putting him centre stage in the way that his father had. The Lambeth Palace archives show how close the courtiers, the archbishop and the chaplains were to the heart of the true seat of power, and how they wanted to manipulate events to shift power back to where it had been when George V was alive. They could be described as Compton's and Gastor's 'King watchers'.

Author Hugo Vickers describes the chaplains as a well-oiled intelligence-gathering machine. In the archive are diary entries by Alexander Sargent, resident chaplain to the Archbishop, who first knew about Mrs Simpson in 1934 when George V referred to Mrs Simpson as "some dreadful common American woman". He complained bitterly that Ernest Simpson appeared to be playing the role of mari complaisant, and that the Simpsons – Ernest and Wallis – had become regular visitors to Fort Belvedere, a house in the grounds of Windsor Castle often used by Edward.

Sargent wrote that "this was common knowledge among people in government and in society and among a good many others too. Servants' talk – I heard a good deal from Walter Wells whose daughter was keeping company with one of the royal chauffeurs – that there are tales of rowdy parties at Fort Belvedere with private cinema showings in Windsor Castle from which they would return in the early hours of the morning… the King was impossible with his staff." Sargent remarks that at that point in 1936 there had been press coverage in the USA about Edward's relationship, but none in the English newspapers.

This sent the Archbishop's private secretary, Alan Don, who turned out to be Lang's conspirator in chief, into a rage: "Our American correspondents have sent us a whole heap of cuttings from the Yankee press which makes one positively sick. Friends say the monarch is deeply in love."

Alan Don wrote in his journal that Edward's own private secretary had been to see Dr Lang. This was highly significant, as Hardinge was building an alliance with Lang: "So far, the English press has been effectively muzzled but there is much talk. We feel as if we are sitting on a volcano. Hardinge was here for a long chat about I know not what, but I can guess!"

Indeed on 13 November, Hardinge wrote to the King warning: "The silence in the British Press on the subject of Your Majesty's friendship with Mrs Simpson is not going to be maintained... Judging by the letters from British subjects living in foreign countries where the Press has been outspoken, the effect will be calamitous." Senior British ministers knew that Hardinge was writing to the King and may have helped him draft the letter.

Dr Susan Williams, in *The People's King*, described the "Old Gang" alarmed by the King's behaviour: "There was horror amongst them. They were afraid of losing influence and power, not having a sense of being at the centre. They felt they had been shunted to the side."

Lang had already begun a process to convince Stanley Baldwin that Edward was 'unfit' to be on the throne. In November 1936, the Archbishop had been speaking in confidence to the Prime Minister about Edward and the "King's Matter" – the euphemism in royal circles and in court for those who were in the know about Mrs Simpson.

Later in an entry into his diary, he wrote: "SECRET... the King's Matter... I had a long talk with Prime Minister Baldwin at Hatfield on I think November 1 1936. He told me that he had an interview with the King and acknowledged his Majesty's desire for domestic happiness and companionship." Lang seemed to be deducing that he could trust Baldwin to steer him towards abdication.

50

And then in October of that year, Alan Don's diary reveals: "Wallis Simpson's accommodating husband has committed adultery in order to give her freedom. What will the sequel be?"

Members of the British Government were further alarmed after being told that Wallis Simpson was allegedly passing documents to the Nazis in Germany. The Foreign Office obtained leaked dispatches from the German Reich's Ambassador to the United Kingdom, Drummond's friend Joachim von Ribbentrop, which revealed his strong view that opposition to the marriage was motivated by the wish "to defeat those Germanophile forces which had been working through Mrs. Simpson". It was rumoured that Simpson had access to confidential government papers sent to Edward, which he left unguarded at his Fort Belvedere residence in the grounds of Windsor Castle. Moreover, FBI files written after the abdication reveal a further series of claims: that during her affair with the King, Simpson was simultaneously having an affair with Ambassador Ribbentrop. The FBI claims were symptomatic of the extremely damaging gossip circulating about the woman Edward proposed to make queen.

So much coming and going, so many lights burning late in the autumn gloom, such banks of fog wrapping round conspiratorial figures flitting round Downing Street, over the bridge to Lambeth Palace, and around Fort Belvedere. No surprise that government ministers ordered the king's phone to be tapped at the house in Windsor Great Park. Meanwhile Mosley, in black military uniform with jackboots was driving round the city inciting trouble, the Jarrow marchers were gathering for a rally in Hyde Park – organised by the

Communist Party – and the Nazis were marching round the Rhineland. To quote Edward, whatever next?

51

The Archbishop and some of 'The Old Gang' met with Stanley Baldwin who announced he was minded to let Edward have his cake and eat it: to maintain his relationship in some form with Mrs Simpson, and still remain king. Why shouldn't a king have a mistress? He wouldn't have been the first frisky monarch.

Dr Lang would have none of it. In those crucial weeks from the beginning of November to December 10, Archbishop Lang had begun in earnest a campaign to ensure the PM would see the error of his suggestion.

This was when Lang recruited Geoffrey Dawson, the editor of the hugely influential London Times into his plotting. Alan Don's diary entry for November 11 reads: "It seems to be agreed that Stanley Baldwin must take action quite soon to clear the air. Dawson is prepared to come out with an utterance in The Times if necessary."

Such a promise was worth its weight in gold. If Lang needed to press the nuclear button and subject Edward to media exposure, then he could. But which particular aspect of Edward's unsuitability for the throne should be exposed?

A memo to Dawson at the Times dated November 12th in which Lang thanked him for the 'confidential talk' the day before, reveals how confident Lang had become: "... it becomes increasingly apparent that some decisive clearing of the air must be achieved in the shortest possible time... I only hope the Prime Minister will now take some further definite steps. I expect he would wish to do so before anything appeared in the Times." The day after receiving this memo, Baldwin authorised a letter to the king warning him that marriage to Mrs Simpson would mean abdication first.

52

Then Churchill stuck his oar in by suggesting that Edward and Mrs Simpson should be allowed to marry, and Mrs S would become the Duchess of Cornwall. Crash went Lang's apple cart. Churchill's intervention, often overlooked in text books because of this embarrassingly pro-Edward stance, had the potential to change the course of history.

Lang believed he had to act immediately, so he wrote a note by hand – he did not have it typed for fear of exposing his plotting. And once again a footman set off across the river with an important message for Downing Street. Lang's 'smoking gun' memo to Baldwin dated November 25th reads as follows: "Forgive me if I seem to intrude unasked. I gather it is becoming more and more difficult to prevent leakage into the Press. If so, the leakage will become a flood and burst the dam. He must leave as soon as possible. The announcement should appear to be a free act. I understand that you are seeing him tonight and doubtless you would make this plain."

On the evening of November 26th, Baldwin did indeed see the King and told him bluntly that his friend Churchill's plan was dead; it would not be tolerated by Downing Street. Historians agree that Lang's intentions are laid bare for all to see – the hand-written note, the hand delivery to Baldwin, the pressure on a Prime Minister he had slowly talked round to his way of thinking. On Channel Four's

The Plot to Topple A King, Dr Susan Williams summarises the situation as a perfect combination of power: "Each person had a particular contribution to offer: Dawson could write pernicious articles about the king; the Archbishop was guardian of the soul and by giving his blessing to a plan, it bathed it in moral rectitude. They were on the right side of history."

53

On December 2nd, what the Establishment had known about Mrs Simpson for months suddenly became public. The Bishop of Bradford made a thinly-veiled attack on the King for not attending church despite being head of the Church of England as monarch. And the press took his attack as referring to Edward's affair with Mrs Simpson.

Alex Sargent's diary reveals Lang very angry that the Bishop of Bradford, Bishop Blunt, had "burst the dam": "Why can't he hold his tongue? If only he knew all that I know..." Sargent thought he protested too much: "There is of course no doubt that he (Lang) did object most strongly to Mrs Simpson, and that he always thought Edward unfit to be king."

To Lang's horror, the popular press initially took the side of the king, and against Lang's stance. There appeared to be enough of a groundswell of support for Edward to survive with Wallis Simpson as his queen. In mid-November, newspapers and the Pathé newsreels reported Edward's unexpected visit to the site of the Dowlais Steel Works in South Wales, the prince claiming to be empathising with the unemployed men who were clearing the site ready to build an 'occupational centre'.

Lang wrote: "...On December 2nd the press published fully an address by the Bishop of Bradford to his diocesan conference in which, after admirably speaking about the significance of the Coronation Service, he spoke of the part of the King in self-dedication and of his need for Divine Grace, adding that it could be wished that he showed more awareness of this need. He explained the next day that the address had been prepared six weeks before and that he had no intention to refer to the rumours which had become current but only to his negligence in church-going.

"But these last words had already been taken as referring to such rumours and proved to be the leakage that at last burst the dam. The Times had a long article on December 3 and the Daily Mail and the News Chronicle ran articles favouring 'the compromise' that aroused public sentiment for the king."

54

But then, manna from heaven.

On December 4 1936, Donald Rea, a vicar living in the village of Eye in Suffolk, contacted Lambeth Palace about a confidential matter: did he know that a qualified psychiatrist who used spirit mediums was treating King Edward for alcoholism and other problems? Archbishop Lang grasped the opportunity with both hands and immediately requested information from a Harley Street doctor to find out about Dr Cannon. He also informed Prime Minister Stanley Baldwin of the news.

A parishioner in the strangely-named village of Eye, a Mrs Bell, had told the vicar she had heard Dr Cannon claiming that he was treating the king for alcoholism. That same day, Archbishop Lang called on the Church of England to offer prayers to the King and his Government. In the press, surprise was expressed about the existence of Mrs Simpson, even though the establishment and their newspaper editors had known for years. And the Lambeth Palace intelligence machine came swinging into action.

Alan Don sent a memo to Dr Lang: "I spoke to the lady who was in touch with the Rev Donald Rea. It concerned the hypnotic treatment of a certain individual for alcoholism. I told her to tell Rev. Rea to put the gist of the matter on paper and to send it here marked "private and confidential" by registered post."

Lang wasted no time, and knew exactly who to turn to – an eminent psychologist whose offices were to be found on Harley Street, literally around the corner from Dr Cannon's second London clinic on Welbeck Street. Psychologist Dr William Brown was already known to Archbishop Lang. Ironically but perhaps very fittingly, Dr Brown was on the panel convened by the Church of England to investigate claims made by spiritualists like Dr Cannon.

For a second time, Brown was to be expert witness, this time to deliver a verdict on Dr Cannon. Lambeth Palace wrote to Rev. Rea to win his co-operation in including Dr Brown in the hasty investigation to find out more about Cannon: "The Archbishop received your letter of December 4. The Archbishop wonders if circumstances rendered it desirable, you or your informant would have any objection to his seeing Dr Brown with a view to ascertaining his opinion of Dr Alexander Cannon, who as you report has been in attendance of his Majesty the King."

There was of course no objection, and so Dr Lang, keeping Baldwin fully informed, fired off the following letter the day before the abdication:

My Dear Brown,

I have been informed by credible persons that a certain Dr Cannon of 53 Welbeck Street has recently been attending the King and that you know something about him. Would you kindly tell me:

1. whether you have reason to suppose that this is true;
2. and whether you think that this Dr Cannon is really a trustworthy person?

He seems from the accounts I have received to be one who encourages somewhat dangerous methods of treatment. I shall of course regard any answer you give as confidential and only for my information.

Yours sincerely,
 Dr Cosmo Lang (Archbishop of Canterbury).

But Lang had also already broken his promise of secrecy. In an effort to smear King Edward, he had instructed Alan Don to write to the editor of the Times, Geoffrey Dawson. It was a letter which as far as Edward was concerned was devastating, and had its roots in the original hypnosis allegations concerning Dr Cannon:

My Dear Dawson,

I have heard from a trustworthy source that His Majesty is mentally ill and that his obsession is due not to mere obstinacy

but to a deranged mind… in the past he has shown symptoms of persecution mania. This would lead almost inevitably to recurring quarrels with his ministers if he remained on the throne.

Sincerely,

Alan Don

The story never appeared of course, but the intention was clear.

In the week between the arrival of the letter from Donald Rea and the abdication on December 10th, Lang was in consultation with Stanley Baldwin on a daily basis, and it seems likely that these communications with Donald Rea brought additional pressures to bear on King Edward in the final hours before he decided to abdicate. For on the morning of Edward's abdication, Alan Don had a very detailed telephone conversation with Dr Brown about Dr Cannon. Usefully for the history books, Dr Brown then wrote to the Archbishop to confirm what had been said to Alan Don, Lang's key co-conspirator.

Significantly, Brown used a similar description of Edward's mental state to that used by Piers Compton in the recording, made in the 1980s – that losing his addiction to alcohol in Edward's case may have been replaced by another fixation – Mrs Simpson. He also made the first official mention of Dr Cannon's psychic assistants, the de Rhonda sisters.

Dr Brown wrote in his letter on December 10th:

My Dear Archbishop,

I write briefly in reply to your confidential letter of yesterday's date – and in confirmation of my telephone conversation with your secretary this morning. I am not personally acquainted with the doctor you mention and have no right to make any criticism of him (apart from on scientific grounds with parts of the only book I have read *"The Invisible Influence"* published by Rider – if you glanced at this book you would probably feel the same about it.)

But a lady, giving the name Mrs Bell, consulted me on November 10th about a relation of hers and described the psychological situation which I recognised as a possible result of the use of hypnotism in treatment of alcoholism and as illustrating the risks in its use unless knowledge and caution are shown. Addiction to alcohol may be replaced by addiction to something else (varying in different cases). She then mentioned this doctor's name and on a subsequent occasion on the telephone she has described to me her own personal visit to him when he put a medium into a trance and (then he) invited her to ask questions of the medium. This was a procedure used by the Marquis de Puységur in 1784 with his somnambulistic subject Victor, but not one that I as a medical psychologist would use at the present day, or consider really useful.

So my report must be hypothetical not categorical and is dependent on statements from Mrs Bell.

I saw Viscount Dawson of Penn (doctor to the royal family)

today and gave him a concise statement of fact in connection with this whole matter.

Yours sincerely,
Dr William Brown.

So whilst Archbishop Lang had sought clarification from Dr Brown, and was still awaiting his official and informed verdict on Dr Cannon, he went ahead and told Baldwin of Cannon's treatment of Edward. He also sanctioned the letter from Don to the Times.

Both of these acts created very definite tipping points in the crisis, putting Edward in a straitjacket, or tightening its grip. And despite the pressures of the aftermath of the abdication, and the pressure of preparing for his own address to the nation, Lang still found time to write back to Dr Brown on the day after abdication. He had to make sure his tracks remained covered. It is clear that he had achieved his goal: there was to be no further inquiry into Dr Cannon to ascertain whether or not his really were 'dangerous treatment methods'.

In Brown's own words, his report was 'hypothetical, not categorical and dependent on statements from Mrs Bell'.

The letter is short and to the point, written less than 24 hours after Edward had gone:

Confidential

Dear Dr Brown. This is only to thank you cordially for your letter in answer to the questions which I ventured to put to you. I do not think this necessary to go further into this painful matter as the issues have now finally been determined. But I am

grateful for the information you have given me.

However, a letter on December 12th from Archbishop Lang to Viscount Dawson, King Edward's doctor, reveals that not only did Stanley Baldwin but also Viscount Dawson wanted to double check the facts about Dr Cannon, as both had requested to see what Lang had discovered about him. Lang again reminds Dawson about the need for secrecy, thereby covering his own tracks:

STRICTLY confidential and private.

My Dear Dawson,

When I saw you this morning I think I promised to send the information about this medical man who is stated to have visited the late King. I have also, as I told you, heard from Dr William Brown about him – very critical. As the Prime Minister would like to see the enclosed document to complete his own analysis of the human situation of one with whom he had such close dealings, even though for the present his responsibilities are over, I should be very grateful if you would jot down your impressions of the document itself. I know well in this matter we must be very careful. But I am sure that as between ourselves and the Prime Minister, confidence can be kept.

Chaplain Alex Sargent's diary entries however raise the real questions hanging over Edward, and why Lang took the action he did, and why 'history was on his side':

"Those who know him (Edward) from the inside regard him as

definitely abnormal, psychologically, if not mentally or physically. Drink or drugs may have contributed to the result, which is that he became a sort of slave to this woman and cannot do without her. It is not a case of normal love but an obsession."

When Archbishop Lang made his subsequent speech, Piers Compton and John Gastor would have pointed to a man they were certain fell into their category of "King Watcher", guilty of conspiracy, but without knowing how right they were. His speech was criticised by some in the press as lacking charity, kicking a man when he was down although whether Edward was deserving of charity is another matter.

Referring to the circle of friends Cannon had worked so hard to share with Edward, Lang said Edward had "surrendered a high and sacred trust from God, confirming the home truth that you pick the friends you deserve. Even more strange and sad it is that he should have sought his happiness in a manner inconsistent with Christian principles of marriage, and within a social circle whose standards and ways of life are alien to all the best instincts and traditions of his people. Let those who belong to this circle know that today they stand rebuked by the judgement of the nation which had loved King Edward. I have shrunk from saying these words but have felt compelled for the sake of truth and sincerity to say them."

55

But, unless their respective story-telling is coloured by hindsight, while Lang's plot was unfolding, the Blackshirts instinctively knew their would-be leader was under threat. Piers Compton describes a meeting just before the abdication at which Edward was revealed to be 'in the grip of England's master of Black Magic'. And so unfolds the Blackshirt version of events on the street, and in the minds of those who wanted to subvert what they saw as an Establishment plot which had involved Dr Cannon all along.

In the Prince of Wales, the fascists had invested a great deal of hope. Almost two years before the 'electrifying events' which ended in abdication (a wounding defeat for the English extreme right), Edward was introduced to Mosley, leader of the British Union of Fascists. They shared many aims and friends. Edward set up a study group to analyse what Mussolini and Hitler were up to – the group would meet for excited talk at the home of Lady Cunard, the woman who was to introduce Wallis Simpson to lots of German Nazis. She thereby created connections which alienated her even more from members of the Establishment who were kept in the loop with MI5 briefings. Mix in political alarm at Edward's inclinations to speak out about issues, and the 'king watchers' were indeed watching Edward and Wallis's every move.

One example of a moment which caused alarm came when word got back to Whitehall was Edward's reaction to a question asked when he had just become king. On January 19th 1936, George V died, and the Duke of Saxe-Coburg Gotha, a Nazi Party member and President of the Anglo-German Fellowship, attended the funeral as Hitler's emissary. He told Edward the Fuhrer wanted friendly relations with Britain and asked him if it would be useful for Hitler and the Prime Minister Stanley Baldwin to meet.

"Who is the King here?" asked Edward. "Baldwin or I? I myself wish to talk to Hitler."

56

In the days running up to abdication, the question at the forefront of some people's minds, not least the king himself, was whether or not he would demand to remain on the throne in some shady alliance with Mosley, sacking Prime Minister Baldwin and thereby, in theory at least, risking what would have been called a fascist coup, albeit probably a very British one. Would he insist on marrying Mrs Simpson and potentially risk trouble on the streets, and somehow draw on strong support from the German and Italian dictators? Or would he simply go quietly?

In the end it was of course the latter. But the process of arriving at his decision had involved a huge amount of political jockeying and negotiations, with threats of civil war being a concern. There was a febrile atmosphere in central London as the crisis made front page news every day. Piers Compton himself spoke of lights burning well into the night across London as neighbours stood on doorsteps debating what should happen, not quite realising the stakes were so high – and what was going through the minds of the far-right and the king himself.

The British Union of Fascists had launched a "Save The King" campaign and, reflecting the tactics deployed by Hitler's special envoy Joachim von Ribbentrop, was drawing on the support of ex-servicemen from the First World War. The right saw the veterans as a powerful political lobby in support of backing the king against Baldwin. The idea of a "King's Party" had been floated by Mosley, and in an often forgotten episode, it more than caught the eye of Winston Churchill. Support for it however evaporated once Edward felt he could not be part of such a radical move. In later years he wrote: "In the end, I put out of my mind the thought of challenging the Prime Minister. By making a stand I should have left the scars of civil war."

On the day the abdication was announced, the newsreel footage focused on the comings and goings at Downing Street and the royal palaces; the Fascists who had gathered outside Buckingham Palace to chant: "One, two, three, four, five, we want Baldwin dead or alive!" did not get a look-in.

It was during the build-up to that final demonstration outside Buckingham Palace that Blackshirt supporter Piers Compton found himself pounding the streets of London. Over a number of days he was to investigate what he saw as the plot to overthrow King Edward.

57

Just to remind ourselves, the story about Dr Cannon's exposure to Lang goes that armed with gossip that the doctor was attending the King, a Mrs Bell had gone to see her local vicar in the Suffolk village of Eye, Donald Rea, and told him of the strange tale and his alleged alcohol problems. Rea then passed the information on to the Archbishop of Canterbury: that the king was being treated by a mystic occultist, Dr Alexander Cannon.

But why did the original tip-off come from such an obscure rural source? How did the Blackshirts get to know about Dr Cannon and then take action to subvert the plot? How were they so quick off the mark? Was this just a Blackshirt urban myth cooked up and somehow pieced together from insider gossip years later?

One possible answer lies in local government records in Suffolk – the accuracy of Compton and Gastor's Cannon accounts becomes more understandable given the fact that there were two Blackshirt councillors in the village of Eye in 1936, and they were sufficiently active to be interned when the war came.

In the The Times dated Friday, June 7th, 1940, the following tale entitled 'Fascist Round-Up': "*It was stated by the police yesterday that four Suffolk officials of the British Union of Fascists have been taken into custody under the Defence Regulations. They are Ronald Noah Creasy and George Frederick Hoggarth, both of Eye, near Ipswich and Lawrence W. Harding and Raymond Smith, both of Bury St Edmunds.*"

Ronald Creasy was in later years after the war remembered as a "quiet old gentleman puttering about on a ride-on mower along the verges outside his manor-style home". In fact he had spent most of the Second World War in prison or prison camps along with some 800 of British fascist Oswald Mosley's leading followers. Amid fears they would assist any Nazi invaders, they were rounded up under defence regulation 18(b) after the fall of France. Police called round at Ronald Creasy's house, just like they did at Captain George Drummond's house in Northampton, and took him away. Where Captain Drummond's royal contacts were to keep him out of the internment camps, Eye councillors Creasy and Hoggarth were banged up without hesitation.

There is of course a possibility that John Gastor spoke to them as part of his post-war research. Certainly in the far-right *Rune* magazine, in an interview with the BNP's Nick Griffin, Ronald Creasy recalls how when he was elected, Oswald Mosley himself came to give thanks to the burghers who had voted for him: "Mosley spoke to enthusiastic crowds at Eye Town Hall."

In the early 1930s, the Fascist movement was strong in the Norfolk and Suffolk borderlands, particularly among farmers, who attracted British Union of Fascist backing in their campaign against the Church of England's demands for 'tithes'.

Tithes were taxes paid to the local church – people paid one tenth of everything they produced. By the 19th Century there was a great deal of resentment towards the payments, particularly from non-Anglicans, who still had to support the church. They were abolished in 1936.

Famously, there were pitched battles between the police and uniformed BUF members outside Wortham rectory in Eye in 1936 where the fascists were picketing. Two Suffolk and Norfolk writers, Doreen Wallace, who wrote *The Tithe Wars* and *East Anglia*, and Henry Williamson, who famously wrote *Tarka the Otter*, were Fascist sympathisers. They helped ensure that the BUF were welcomed locally.

58

So there is a clear route from the original Cannon gossip being communicated to Archbishop Lang, and the same gossip will have been communicated through the Blackshirt network to people like Piers Compton and the broader Fascist movement in London which was ready to pounce on any news which could be construed as a government conspiracy against their king. Suspicions will have been confirmed by whispers that 'the King was in the grip of a master of Black Magic'.

Indeed, on December 10th 1936, hours before Edward's abdication speech, and hours after the Abdication Bill had been announced in both Houses of Parliament, the police flooded central London with officers as Special Branch were fearful of a riot which would have been led by the Blackshirts, furious their King was about to abdicate. To them there was the whiff of conspiracy lurking in the air. They had longed for Edward to be King and their leader Sir Oswald Mosley to be Prime Minister. Up until early December 1936, Mosley believed he was within a whisker of power, and that he had the backing of the country.

So convinced was Piers Compton that Cannon was knowingly complicit in conspiracy, Piers says in the recording that he went to visit Dr Cannon in an attempt to find out more about him, working his way to him through a network of London society characters: someone who knew someone, who knew someone else. His memory in the recording, which as we know dates back to 1985, appears to be as clear as a whistle. It is obviously a story, at the time almost 50 years old, which he believed whole-heartedly.

59

Conspiratorial from the start, the recording begins by Compton revealing he was a member of a secret organisation which he does not name, but he does describe.

It is possible to guess that it was the Imperial Policy Group, a right-wing group of appeasers which argued that Britain should stay out of European conflicts, most certainly appease and work with

Hitler, but concentrate on its empire and rebuild Britain's economic and political power via the colonies.

He says there were some extremely notable, but absent, supporters who only ever sent their minions to meetings: "It was quite the most influential movement so far as prominent people are concerned. It occupied one floor of what was known as British Industries House, which was at the Marble Arch end of Oxford Street. When I last passed it I saw it was the C&A building. Who financed it I am not quite sure. One of the men who did was Sir Harry Brittain (wealthy former politician and journalist). The movement was designed to strengthen our links with the colonies and to avert the coming war.

"It was supported in an underground way by Neville Chamberlain... he was not a great man of course: he meant well, but he was rather weak and never dared appear there... The man we had to deal with was Sir Charles Morgan Webb... Chamberlain's financial adviser to the House of Lords." In the recording, he gives a unique view on why the Blackshirts had put so much hope in the man they hoped would be leader.

"The Germans certainly believed Edward was going to form an alliance with them when he became King. Ribbentrop said as much at an Anglo German dinner which was attended by Edward when he said at the end, "I think we should need a dictator here before long." That was all interpreted as going along the same Nazi line.

Compton continued, "The movement I was in used to receive an extraordinary lot of absolutely reliable information. I was the one who used to follow it up."

Out of all the tip-offs, the one about Dr Cannon was the most noteworthy and deserving of fast action because the abdication crisis appeared to be completely unpredictable. Compton, as a journalist with contacts in every national newspaper and throughout 'high society', was best placed to undertake this task.

60

There are a number of moments in Compton's recording when he names people who witnessed massive moments in history. One such person was Meriel Buchanan Knowling, the daughter of Sir George Buchanan, Britain's amabassador to Russia at the time of the Bolshevik Revolution. He had developed a strong bond with the Tsar Nicholas II and attempted to convince the Tsar that granting some constitutional reform would stave-off revolution. He failed, and was later criticised for failing to ensure safe passage out of Russia for the Russian royals. It is now known that this was not his fault but that of the Tsar's first cousin King George V who, fearful of revolutionary trends in Britain and the stability of his own throne, persuaded the Lloyd George government to rescind the offer they had made to provide sanctuary for the Imperial Family.

A story of survival amid the chaos of revolution is included in Meriel Buchanan Knowling's own book *Ambassador's Daughter*.

The Romanovs, the Russian royal family famously executed by the Bolsheviks, had troubles of their own with a mystic in their midst. This was Rasputin, who had reputedly used hypnotherapy on the young prince Alexei who had haemophilia, a genetically inherited condition common amongst members of the royal families of Europe. He apparently successfully eased the boy's symptoms, and was declared a healer. He set himself up as the "Mad Monk" psychic and occultist.

Like Dr Cannon, Rasputin was said to have a "grip" on certain royals. Ironically, Sir George Buchanan happened to be in the same room to hear claims put to Tsar Nicholas that Rasputin's murder in 1916 had not been carried out by a Russian, but by an Englishman.

61

So it was with further irony that Meriel Buchanan Knowling was around when another mystic had suddenly popped up in close proximity to a royal – this time she was to hand his name and address to Piers Compton to investigate him.

"Mrs Buchanan Knowling, who was quite a well-known figure in London society at the time, telephoned me and invited me to go along to Leicester Square to see her. There I found a group of men who had been with Buchanan in Russia."

Compton described Mrs Buchanan Knowling standing alongside a group of men pulling a lot of documents out of a box and looking through them: "They told me that Edward Prince of Wales was in the grip of a man, a famous man in his way, a leader of Black Magic in England... They gave me his name and address, the story was that this black magician had been called in to treat Edward for drunkenness."

Then Compton describes Edward's problem in exactly the way Dr William Brown described it to Archbishop Lang: "Now it's a well-known fact that when you drive one weakness such as a drug out of a person, another weakness takes its place... and the story told to me was whereas he was partly cured of drunkenness, he was wholly dependent on a woman who had taken the place of that drink. Mrs Simpson first appeared in London life in October 1934, and by May 1935 she was being openly named in the lighter newspapers as the Prince of Wales's girl. She ousted Mrs Dudley Ward in his affections and took complete possession of him. He would never make a decision without consulting Mrs Simpson. If she was not there he was quite helpless and when he called for her and she was not there he would threaten suicide. He simply could not be without it – or her – I should say."

Compton laughed, embarrassed by his faux pas.

"This Alexander Cannon had started life in London as an ordinary doctor and had committed some misdemeanor and had been struck off the rolls."

So back in 1936, Compton knew quite a lot about this man who was treating the king for alcoholism, who had indeed been sacked from Colney Hatch. He knew there was an unexplained 18-month gap in General Medical Council records before Dr Cannon re-appeared as a practitioner in the Harley Street district of London. Mirroring the MI5 file on Cannon, Compton says: "He vanished and no-one knows quite where he went until he came to number 22 to 24 Welbeck Street (in fact number 53) and a number of well-known people went to him for treatment.

"So hearing this, I was all agog. The air was electric in London, I felt I was getting into things. I went right away to Welbeck Street to see him."

62

It was late evening by the time Piers Compton arrived at Dr Cannon's premises at Welbeck Street. The building is now home to The Society of Chiropodists and Podiatrists, a travel agents and a management agency of some kind. But in late 1939, MI5 reckoned

Dr Cannon occupied the whole building, and from what Compton says in the recording, they were right. Compton described himself as being on a mission – that the future of the monarchy and Empire or at least the Fascist view of how they were to be preserved – rested on his shoulders. His head was buzzing with the moment.

And Piers Compton and his Blackshirt compatriots were not alone. Mosley and the King received the support of press baron Lord Rothermere, owner of the *Daily Mail* and the *Evening News*. On January 8th, 1934, the Mail carried the front page headline "Hurrah for the Blackshirts!" Mosley's followers had donned Blackshirts aping other Fascist uniforms.

After Edward's visit to poverty stricken Wales in November 1936, not long before the Edward and Mrs Simpson crisis hit the headlines, one executive of the Daily Mail wrote: "The suggestion has been made that Edward could, if he wished, make himself the Dictator of the Empire. Some minds see in his South Wales activity and brusqueness a sign that he may yet dominate the politicians."

For Sir Henry 'Chips' Channon, chronicler of the abdication crisis from the point of view of the gin-swilling smart set, Edward was pro-German, while the Blackshirts regarded him as a 'member of the war (WWI) generation, a kindred spirit'.

With his head filled with these ideas, Piers Compton marched through the streets of London on that cold, dark night, to Welbeck Street, becoming more and more concerned about what to do if Cannon put him 'into a trance'.

The ambassador's daughter Meriel Buchanan Knowling had given him some advice about fending him off if he deployed his occult powers. "If you can go armed… do so… and if you feel yourself going into a trance when you are talking to him, don't hesitate to shoot him!"

He did not say if he was armed or not, but he was troubled by not having an appointment: "As you can imagine, you can't see anyone in that part of London without an appointment and it was fairly late at night.

"I rang the bell and it was opened by a typical housekeeper dressed all in black and I asked to see Dr Alexander Cannon… I was told it wasn't possible, but I was like a very persistent salesman, I put my foot in the door and said I must see him as I had something very important to ask him."

"She argued a bit and as we were arguing… it was quite a long hall, and I could see a staircase at the end and I was suddenly aware that a man's legs were coming down to the hall. He stood there and waited while I was still arguing with the housekeeper, and then I heard him say suddenly, 'Let him in'"

He was finally in the wolf's lair – a Blackshirt inside the clinic of the man who possibly knew intimate details of the King's drinking and sexual problems, the man whose activities those Blackshirts saw as threatening the man who could have saved Britain and the Empire from the Red Bolshevik Peril.

"I was shown into a room which was lined from floor to ceiling with books. I was there for five to ten minutes I would guess. I had a strange impression I was being watched all the time. I looked around at the titles of the books. Some of them were about magic, Tibet and similar subjects. One I took down had a front picture of Dr A Cannon in what we would call mandarin robes. The caption described him as the grandmaster of the Great White Lodge of the Himalayas.

"I was eventually shown into a consulting room with a couch in the corner, and he asked me what I wanted. He did not know how much I knew. For quite a long time we just fenced with words. It was the most difficult time I had had in my life because I could say nothing definite. And I did not want to put him off to let him know that I was ignorant of the heart of the matter."

"Presently I pointed to the psychiatrist's couch and I said: 'I understand you have some very well-known clients.'

"I should describe him at this point as half Chiny half Jew," – revealing his Blackshirt racism – "Tall, bald and very broad, a big head, with what hair he had pulled tight... He stood with his hands folded over his chest... When I said 'You have a number of prominent people as patients,' he replied, 'I have that honour'."

So I ran off one or two of the names that I had been told – names straight from Who's Who of London society, from all sides of the political spectrum, an eclectic mix of characters at the forefront of political thinking – mostly right-wing, but some on the left. They were a foretaste of the colourful characters to be found in Cannon's clinic in the 1940s on the Isle of Man, alongside military admirals and commanders.

Compton started a brief roll call: "I named Mrs Victor Gollancz. Cannon leant forward and said, 'I have that honour.' He used that word 'honour' a lot."

(Victor Gollancz formed his own publishing company in 1927 and set up The Left Book Club, publishing works by writers such as George Orwell. In addition to his highly successful publishing, Gollancz was a prolific writer on a variety of subjects. The Left Book Club was not only a book club run along commercial lines, but also a campaigning group that aimed to propagate left wing ideas in Britain.

Gollancz was one of the foremost British campaigners during the Second World War on the issue of the Nazi extermination of European Jews. In the summer of 1942 Gollancz was to realise that he and the rest of the world had been seriously underestimating the extent of the Nazi persecution of the Jews. He explained in his 16,000 word pamphlet Let My People Go, written over Christmas 1942, that between one and two million Jews had already been murdered in Nazi-controlled Europe and "unless something effective is done, within a very few months these six million Jews will all be dead.")

Another long-standing patient was the anti-capital punishment campaigner Violet Van der Elst, a woman he spoke up for in court in early 1936 when she was fined £3 'for refusing to stop her car' during demonstrations which turned violent outside a Manchester prison where an execution had taken place.

The daughter of a coal porter and a washerwoman, she became a successful businesswoman by developing Shavex, the first brush-less shaving cream. In the 1930s she married Jean Van der Elst, a Belgian painter. Having amassed a huge personal fortune she purchased Harlaxton Manor, in Lincolnshire, and gained publicity from her vocal campaigns against capital punishment, and stood three times, unsuccessfully, as a Labour Party candidate to be an MP.

There then came from Compton's mouth the name of someone from the opposite side of the political spectrum.

'Lady Duff Cooper'... and Cannon again bowed and said: "I have that honour."

Born Lady Diana Olivia Winifred Maud Manners, she was officially the youngest daughter of the 8th Duke of Rutland and his wife, the former Violet Lindsay, but Lady Diana's real father was widely supposed to be the writer, Henry Cust. In her prime, she mixed with royals – and her parents had once had high hopes she would marry an HRH herself – in fact the one who turned out to be a fellow Cannon patient himself.

She had the widespread reputation as the most beautiful young woman in England, and appeared in countless profiles, photographs and articles in newspapers and magazines. She became active in The Coterie, an influential group of young English aristocrats and intellectuals of the 1910s whose prominence and numbers were cut short by the First World War. Lady Diana was the most famous of the group, but it included Raymond Asquith, son of HH Asquith the Prime Minister, Patrick Shaw Stewart, Edward Horner, Sir Denis Anson and Duff Cooper. Following the sudden deaths of Asquith, Horner, Shaw-Stewart, and Anson – the first three in the war; Anson by drowning – Lady Diana married Cooper, one of the last surviving male members of her circle of friends, in June 1919. It was not a popular choice in the Manners household. Whether Cannon was hypnotizing The Lady Diana Cooper for her famously narcissistic tendencies we will never know.

But in Cannon's clinic on that night in December 1936, with Edward only a day or two from abdicating, deliberating what the future may hold for him, Compton "fenced with words", as he continued to dig for the truth about who he was treating.

"Then quick as lightening I said: 'Edward Prince of Wales!'"

"And he bent forward slightly and said: 'Who told you that?'"

"Then he reverted to his former static attitude but that had broken his thoughts somewhat. He felt I knew much more than I did. I said I wanted to write an article for the newspapers. Of course I lied and said I would show him it before publishing. It was an oppressive atmosphere. I certainly felt very strange there."

Secure in the knowledge that he had confirmation of what he feared, Compton did not submit him to any further questioning and left Welbeck Street saying, "I was full of ideas which I had to do something about."

63

"We had a number of meeting places across London – one was a house in Cornwall Gardens. I went straight there and there were people in a meeting. As I said, at that time, people hardly went to bed – the whole place was electric. When they heard what I had to say, they called one or two people. One of them was the Archbishop of Canterbury's private secretary (Alan Don) who apparently knew much more than people do nowadays." (Remember – Compton was talking in the 1980s).

Alan Don was the man Lang had authorised to write a letter to the Times about Edward's questionable sanity. Rightly or wrongly, Don had also participated in Lang's long-term aim of toppling Edward. Another telephone call was to Lady Mary Hope, who was one of Lord Linlithgow's daughters, and a lady in waiting to the Duchess of Kent. Compton says, 'She also used to masquerade as a school mistress and run a building as a school in West Kensington when really she was working with the organization I have mentioned.' Compton claims she put her royal contacts to good use. Edward was holed up in Fort Belvedere, and she called presumably to find out more about the Cannon story. In her phone calls, Lady Mary could not get past Lord Dawson of Penn – as Compton refers to him. Viscount Penn was physician to the royals. Compton says:

"I think it was she who told me that there was someone called Dr Jones waiting to interview the king. Well naturally I thought it was a fake name – but later I wondered whether it had in fact been Dr Jones, Freud's biographer – so he may have been genuine."

Compton describes what was the lead-up to the abdication, with the royal doctor 'standing guard' over Edward. The archives at Lambeth Palace confirm he had become "quite deranged". With Lady Mary's calls getting nowhere, they did not know where to turn: "I was feeling rather desperate at the time."

64

Having tapped into his own Establishment contacts in his attempt to influence the course of history, Compton then claimed he wanted to tip off the newspapers about the fact that the King was 'in the grip of a Black Magic hypnotist', thinking that this would provoke outrage and save Edward from any further influence.

"It was late at night, but I rushed along to Marble Arch, then walked the length of Fleet Street. Having worked there myself I had contacts there. I saw the news editors and literary editors of practically every national newspaper and periodical. I told them the story – that the king was in the grip of a master of Black Magic in England – and they were too frightened to touch it. I finished by resorting to the religious papers. I could see that people were frightened by it.

"Then I had a stroke of luck in the form of Father Grimley, (editor of the Catholic Times). He clapped his hands and said, 'I know all about that.' He was eventually to publish a story 'Moneyed Plot Against The King'. He (Father Grimley) was later got rid of – he was replaced quickly, and the story never really got anywhere."

My attempts to track down a copy of the article have failed.

65

After drawing a blank with Fleet Street and sensing that the end was nigh, Compton decided to call on an old friend – Sir Oswald Mosley, knowing that Mosley was totally committed to Edward remaining on the throne. His party, the British Union, had stated: "He who insults the British Crown thus insults the history and achievement of the British race. The King has been loyal and true to us. My simple demand is that we must be loyal and true to him. The recompense of his country for his twenty five years' faithful service is the denial of every man's right to live in private happiness with the woman he loves. Let the man who has never loved be the first to cast the stone."

With those words rattling in his head, with all options apparently exhausted – and desperate to break to Sir Oswald the news about Cannon – he went to see him at 3am at his headquarters to hatch a plan to subvert what he saw as unfolding in front of him. He wanted to publicize what he had found out about Dr Cannon and 'rescue' the King.

"I knew Mosley quite well – I had worked with him some years before. He had a hypnotic influence on me. His eyes swiveled and unless you kept tight control of yourself you could have fallen under his influence. It was quite a sensation – he tried it on me most of the time I was talking. I was full of mad schemes. I said, 'Do you have access to a printing press? – I will go round scattering leaflets.'"

Mosley listened to Compton and sat for a while taking stock of what had happened.

"I said I would scatter the leaflets from the roof of the Pavilion Theatre, but he would not agree to that. I asked if he would agree to his defence force... a group of very dedicated men, very tough, who were sworn to do anything – and raid Sunningdale where Edward was staying and carry him off and take him to this Dr Jones to see what had happened to him.

"He humoured me – I realized he was just humouring me – by calling the men together. But we did go down to Sunningdale in a number of cars and small lorries. I think we stayed a mile and a half from Sunningdale because it was very closely guarded at the time and they went forward and dispatched someone to the house.

"I don't know what means they had of getting through, whether it was genuine or not – but someone was dispatched and came back with the news that Squadron Leader Fielden who was at the time commander of the King's Flight told them, 'Don't attempt to do anything because they are going to shoot the King and say that you did it.' So Mosley backed down, and it came to nothing."

Compton and Mosley's mission – if it ever happened exactly as described here – had failed. History books would have of course reflected those events had they been confirmed by other more significant sources. But a cursory check does in fact reveal that Squadron Leader Fielden was indeed chosen by Edward to be his pilot. There is always the possibility he was describing what someone else had witnessed and, in the mists of time, picked up other bits of information and created his story.

But the account is detailed, and the characters involved not so well-known. What is interesting too is that the description of Edward's alcohol addiction being 'replaced by Mrs Simpson' is mentioned in those terms not only by Piers Compton, but Dr William Brown as well.

66

Whether or not the events he described actually took place *exactly* as described seems unlikely. It is only in very recent years that Compton's and Gastor's overall take on events has been confirmed as fairly accurate. The Blackshirt view of the plot seems to hold water. Piers Compton the participant and Gastor the researcher picked up the Cannon story directly after the war with remarkable accuracy. He even spoke to fellow fascists who adhered to a different way of thinking about the story – that having a king under the control of 'Black Magic' would have been dangerous for England.

In his recording, Gastor provides the historical analysis which saw him conclude not only that Cannon was the 'mechanism' by which Edward was toppled off the throne, but also, crucially, Gastor also provides evidence for the second part of the Cannon story – that during the Second World War, Cannon's "hypnotic and occultist powers continued to be taken seriously as he had the backing of the most important elements in Admiralty intelligence".

Gastor's king watcher theory mirrors closely those only very recently expounded by historians Susan William, who wrote *The People's King*, and Hugo Vickers, who wrote *Behind Closed Doors*. They refer to the King Watchers as "the Old Gang", a group of establishment grandees who had hoped to be able to mould Edward into the monarch they wanted. In Gastor's view Edward's knowledge of German language and poetry, and his pro-Nazi politics, meant the grandees had to keep an even closer eye on him.

"As in chess, as in real history, kings, even when they are democratic, are people of enormous and decisive influence. They are in a position to quickly overrule all kinds of oppositions and swing people round. Hence for any democratic and liberalistic system so long as the monarchy is there, there is always the possibility that the monarch can determine to become more absolute and rule affairs. Now with Edward VIII, I think this had happened on account of the danger he represented by his original – and since early upbringing – pro-German attitude in life. It is not the kings who are important. It is the king watchers, they are very important, watching that the kings should not assert themselves.

"As we know from the memoirs of the Polish ambassador Rajinsky, Edward VIII was known to differ from the establishment because he believed in a lasting settlement (with Germany). Already before the abdication crisis, the despatches of the Polish ambassador have also now been published and the pro-German orientation (of the king) and the potential employment of the English monarchy as the greatest factor of a rapprochement with Germany was an omnipresent threat to all those who wanted to clear out all questions of good relationships with Germany."

Gastor concludes that had Edward been 'well-behaved', the King Watchers could not have acted in the way that they did; he also says it was remarkable that despite so many knowing about Dr Cannon and what he was up to with the king, the story about his role never emerged. In recalling the events of 1936, he says: "Lady Mosley and Oswald Mosley in their time in Paris fail in all their memoirs to recall any of these insights about the black magical ties which had been made like a sling around the throat of Edward VIII and which were the mechanism, which made it possible for the establishment to dethrone him, because of course if he had been an entirely well-behaved monarch, they would not have had any purchase over him."

67

A key part of the Cannon story is that on a number of occasions spanning six years, representatives of the secret service, the fascists and possibly even Stanley Baldwin had been sent in undercover to Cannon's clinic to see what he was up to without Cannon realising.

Gastor reveals that Piers Compton was not alone in wanting to infiltrate the clinic to find out who he was, and what exactly was going on in his practice. One of those Cannon clinic infiltrators was the cousin of a man who was certainly very interested in Dr Cannon: Prime Minister Stanley Baldwin. The cousin was a former journalist who worked for the Northcliffe press: "Miss Mary Stanford," said Gastor, "was a lady of high society and birth".

Gastor counted her as one of his Nazi-sympathising contacts. "In 1945, people I met confirmed all that the historian Mr Compton recalls about Dr Cannon from his active participation in the days of the crisis. They were confirmed to me, particularly by Miss Mary Stanford.

"To my amazed surprise, when I said what a tragedy that Edward VIII did not remain on the throne, she said yes, that is what they all think - and it is natural that you should think that, because he was potentially a great enemy of communism and a great friend of Germany.

"BUT! (She said) because of this he had been entrapped and ensnared by the 'King Watchers' who knew he was dangerous. And the instrument was one of a group of black magic osteopaths established in Austria who later moved to London. The head of it was a quack doctor called Alexander Cannon."

Gastor continued: "I myself, said the lady informing me, Miss Mary Stanford, have investigated the clinic of Dr Cannon. It was there on the corner of Welbeck Street and Wimpole Street, and she had penetrated deeply into the activities there. She said that the king was possibly being poisoned, it was possibly being introduced to his brain through ear treatment. She stated it would have been a terrible danger to England if a man under the control of black magicians could have become king."

Gastor claimed that Edward and Dr Cannon had first got to know each other in Vienna where he studied for an M.D., and that they had met up again in London when he re-established his clinic on Harley Street and then Welbeck Street. The original arrangement had been made in Austria because he needed a dry out cure for addictive drinking. But bit by bit, he had become immersed in a world of black magic and sexual yogic activities.

No such story ever appeared about the unsavoury side of the abdication crisis, and neither had the Mrs Simpson story until the last moment. Neither for that matter, the strange story about the king, the hypnotist and the unhealthy influence he held over the king, all evidence said Gastor of an overly compliant media.

"One should conclude from the examination of the subject that the power of the media to suppress facts is quite enormous. I met numerous persons of the pre-war generation who were well versed in these backgrounds who have confirmed to me all aspects of what has been stated to me by Mr Piers Compton."

Not only was it the British media who knew about so many things which it did not publish, it was the German media too. But Gastor could not tame his respect for the Nazi regime and heaps praise on the Germans for keeping schtum about such unsavoury matters as tantric sex: "That all this was known to the German embassy (in Vienna), and journalist Mary Stanford had sent detailed stories to Germany on these matters, the excellent courtesy of the Nazi press towards the British royal family by not expounding this very unsavoury side of the abdication crisis was a sign of the admirable and chivalrous conduct – typical, as she thought, of the then German government."

68

What follows opens a door on a little known aspect of the war – investigations (amounting to more than a passing interest) into what the occult may have offered as a weapon in the Second World War.

Gastor's account takes the Cannon story over to the Isle of Man, complete with clinic, the psychic sisters Rhonda and Joyce de Rhonda, and a Drummonds Bank account increasingly groaning with money from the wartime government, payments to 'treat' war weary officers and commanders.

Gastor mentions aspects of the story which are confirmed by the MI5 file found on the Isle of Man. Then, he intriguingly merely mentions in passing a couple of names and locations, enough for additional research to track down the full story of how Dr Cannon attempted to teach telepathy and promote it as a viable weapon in the battlefield.

He mentions a raid on the Lofoten Islands in Norway's part of the Arctic Circle, and Cannon's activities not only in his clinic, but also at Peveril Camp for fascist internees on the Isle of Man. All figured in what they told him. He said that the prisoners confirmed what Piers Compton had told his son Blaise in the recording, and repeats his bafflement as to how it had been kept secret for so long.

"I should add that Dr Alexander Cannon did not vanish from the scene but continued as a person of prime importance during the Second World War and that his hypnotic and occult powers were taken seriously to such an extent one assumed that he was at the very top of Admiralty intelligence. Admiral Sir Roger Keyes in an article published in 1945 or 1946 just after the end of the war published in the Daily Telegraph, or possibly the Times, stated himself that the raids on the Lofoten Islands undertaken by the Admiralty intelligence with commanders, had been executed under the occult supervision of precisely Dr Alexander Cannon.

"Meantime Alexander Cannon was resident upon the Isle of Man, and a building which appeared to belong to him was used as a screening station for 18b internees who had been brought to the Isle of Man because they had been suspected – in many cases rightly in other cases wrongly – of being pro-German agents or persons who would have liked to have established a conciliatory regime to terminate the ruinous prospects of Bolshevik victory through the period of the Second World War."

Gastor spoke in endless sentences: "Now one such person was a brilliant economist, a lecturer called HT Mills. He claimed that he was in a room belonging to Cannon, established in the Peel concentration camp, and that he was later taken to a room which, from his knowledge of occult things, was certain to have been at one time a black magical temple, and was decorated with numerous black magical symbols, and he related this to the fact that apparently Cannon was screening all arrivals in the Isle of Man." So unfolds part two of the story of Dr Cannon, which shifts from London to the Isle of Man.

Blaise, in the tape recording, asks just one question: "Was Cannon using hypnosis... and drugs?"

And Gastor replies: "One must assume that he was using both hypnosis and drugs. The supposition is that a key factor in the treatment at the clinic in Welbeck Street was an ear treatment. The fact that a ritual temple was involved was divulged to me by the same economist HT Mills who had a considerable file of papers about the lodge of Dr Alexander Cannon. It would appear therefore that wherever he came from, he had the backing of the most important elements in British intelligence which again and again relates to occult personalities. Four or five of the most celebrated agents of the Second World War were occultists and Dr Alexander Cannon (on the Isle of Man) appears to have been a man of authority amongst these people: a master."

69

In the blistering heat of the Isle of Man's summer of 1939, war was hard to imagine. The beaches were packed, the horses sweating as they pulled yet another packed tram load along the bustling promenade which stretches the two-mile length of Douglas Bay.

Before the collapse of the Irish Sea's fish stocks, huge shoals of mackerel and herring could be seen around Douglas harbour. At certain times of the year you could scoop up bucketfuls of baby herring down on the beaches. Basking sharks are still regular visitors. These were the days of coal – the skies above the harbour filled every now and again with huge drifting clouds of black soot, as ferry after ferry deposited thousands of holiday makers at the end of what is one of the most beautiful bays in Europe. They travelled there from across the north of Britain. Life was good. War was a million miles away.

Hard to imagine nine months later that those same ferries were saving lives in the thick of the action on the beaches at Dunkirk. Eight of the Isle of Man Steam Packet Company's boats took part in the Dunkirk evacuation. By the end of the operation, they had rescued a total of 24,699 men, 1 in 14 of those evacuated from Dunkirk. Another reason why tourism came to an abrupt end was because a proportion of the promenade and some of the hotels on it were sealed off with barbed wire and watch tower guns trained on the internees in the hotels.

The island was also a place where the military could come to train, to relax and recoup, get over the horrors of war. The military could also indulge in research which went way off piste – it was as if someone had tipped him the nod about the nature of what would be based on the island, as Dr Cannon was only too willing to invest what was then a fortune by opening The Isle of Man Clinic for Nervous Disorders, a name with more than an echo of Mel Brooks' clinic in *High Anxiety*. It was an occult research institute, an 'assessment' centre, rest home with a psychiatric element, and health spa, all rolled into one. Military patients and wealthy clients received 'treatments' and indulged in the Second World War equivalent of 'blue-sky thinking' about waging war, with lots of eating and drinking thrown in for the not inconsiderable price.

London-focused media overlook the role of the Isle of Man in the war. It was significant not only because it was a secure island full of boats and hotel accommodation, ideal for people you might want to isolate for whatever reason, but also because the Luftwaffe was not particularly interested in reaching it. Training in, and the development of, top secret new technologies such as radar could continue unhindered. But now these revelations of cutting edge research of the Cannon variety add a whole new dimension, particularly as Churchill was said to have had more than a passing interest in 'mind control' and the occult. Cannon boasted of a close relationship with the PM which everyone assumed was a lie. But was he in fact telling the truth?

The clinic was to become unique in the history of war for what happened there, for the range of amazing characters who gathered there, and for how seriously Dr Cannon was taken by the military.

70

Thirty two miles long and 14 miles wide, the Isle of Man stands equi-distant between Ireland and England, a four-hour Steam Packet journey from Liverpool. Aside from its exotic marine life and rugged coastal and mountain scenery, the island was famous in past centuries for smugglers; in more recent centuries for those escaping past lives or tax bills around the world. The island has its own government and budgets and, contrary to what most English people understand, it is largely independent of London.

The island is a tax haven, so if you are Manx, it is completely normal to have a neighbour with a notable past. World famous stars can be spotted on the beaches or in restaurants around the island. The notables might be notable for the wrong reasons, perhaps on the run following some fraud or other, or may be an old rock star, or a loud, old colonial type, trying to protect some semblance of high life from British tax authorities. For a proliferation of characters with a past, the 1930s and 1940s were no different. Dr Cannon and George Drummond found fittingly grand houses on the island at exactly the same time as each other, and they fitted extraordinarily well into this category of quirky 'come-over with a past'. With knobs on, in fact.

To the Manx, Dr Cannon will have been simply another 'dooinney quaagh', which as we know in the native Manx language means 'a weirdo' (phon: 'dun-yuha kwair-kk) – or strange man.

From the start of the war, the island's population swelled as military training centres, RAF bases and prison camps were sited there. The fine sweep of hotels and guest houses built along Douglas bay's two mile promenade saw sections cordoned off with barbed wire, watch towers erected around them, internees and prisoners of war replacing the visitors who had vanished by then. Prisoners and internees were housed in other towns on the island as well. Corresponding to that militarization was an increase in numbers of security service personnel.

Those personnel had to assume spies were everywhere, and they kept an eye on anywhere people gathered, but some locations warranted more attention than others. In Douglas few hotels could hold a candle to the Falcon Cliff for exotic folk. Now an office complex, it overlooks Douglas bay from a dramatic vantage point 250 feet above the promenade. Look up at almost any point along the promenade and you can see the Falcon Cliff, a fittingly exotic building where Dr Cannon and his female companions must have felt at home. Captain Drummond stayed there as well for some time at the start of the war, crammed full of Britain's rich and famous, music hall celebrities, and international TT motorbike racers during the summer.

Rhonda de Rhonda had written to Falcon Cliff proprietor Mrs Ellen Kane in the summer of 1939: would she be good enough to provide accommodation for himself and his two lady assistants for a property searching week from August 13th? Mrs Kane had never before received a letter from a man whose name, and the letters attached to it, spread over four lines from one margin to the other. She hesitated before answering, thinking such a person must be far too grand for her to look after.

Property scout to the rich, hotelier Mrs Kane could see she might lose all her 1939 bookings for September's Grand Prix motor bike races: a disaster. For the last thirty years, the island had been invaded by motor cycling enthusiasts from all over the world, mad to chase each other at astonishing speeds round a 32 mile circuit. Truly international, it had come to be dominated by French, German and Italian built bikes. A German had won the Senior T.T. race that year. He had stayed at the Falcon Cliff. All the team had stayed there. Ellen had booked them in twice a year for the last dozen years. Her very best customers.

A leader column had appeared in The Isle of Man Times, worrying that continuing with the TT in the run-up to war was not wise given the state of European politics. Germans and Italian cycles should be barred along with the German and Italian teams. They might be spies.

Ellen was horrified. But in no time, the island's Governor, Admiral Lord Granville, who liked to call in at her bar most mornings for a quick one on his way to his office, publicly deplored this stance. He wrote to the editor, saying 'politics should not besmirch sport.' He was married to Lady Rose, sister of the Queen Mother. Ellen was delighted to have royal support.

Not that royal approval for a quick stiff drink made any difference. The military was going to requisition almost all boarding houses and hotels as billets for officers setting up wartime bases. Landladies who had got used to charging between 8/6d and 10/6d for a room, breakfast, lunch, tea, late dinner and supper were going to get a lot less from the military.

71

Having booked rooms at the Falcon Cliff, Dr Cannon made the most of his film-star arrival when he first stepped on to Manx soil, doing his best to dramatically sweep down three flimsy, rotting wooden steps which had been wheeled over to the tiny aeroplane. He informed the attending customs inspector that Mrs Ellen Kane had accommodation waiting for him.

One officer described him as "simply the most bizarre character we had ever seen" in his old-fashioned frock coat, batwing collared shirt, large black bow tie and spats: "Mr Pickwick", mopping his face with a huge handkerchief because the temperature was in the 70's. His two assistants were identically dressed – pill box hats at jaunty angles, short, flared skirts, high heeled shoes with peep toes, immaculate make-up.

The assistants announced in unison: 'Your excellency…' bowing in front of their lord and master.

A despatch was immediately addressed to Special Branch at Marylebone, London, from the Isle of Man Security Service. It read: "Staying at a hotel in this town on the Isle of Man is a man who gave his name as Sir Dr Alexander Cannon, KGCP, KCHB, Bart etc, aged about fifty, hair going grey, nearly bald, stout built, well spoken, well dressed. Dr Cannon is accompanied by two young ladies, the 1st Dame Rhonda de Rhonda, Dame of St Hubert, FRGS, the 2nd Joyce de Rhonda, also Dame of St Hubert, FRGS, supposed sister or daughter of the first. These ladies gave their address as 53 Welbeck Street, London."

The officer urged: "Will you please have inquiries made at Welbeck Street (location of Dr Cannon's clinic) as to what is known of these persons and telephone the result as soon as possible? No offence has been committed so far, but they are definitely regarded with suspicion."

72

Cannon the showman had landed on his feet by staying at the Kanes' hotel. A showbiz family through and through, they were also deeply practical organisers. Eva, their only child, was for me a cracking source of information about Cannon.

Her parents helped lay the foundations of the rest of his life on the Isle of Man by initially finding the large house which Dr Cannon called 'Ballamoar Castle', adding the word castle to add grandeur. The Kanes did the same for George Drummond – his palatial home was called 'Mount Rule' in the south of the island.

Eva referred to Cannon simply as 'Doctor'. She was in her mid-teens in 1939, and her mother had taken her away from school, insisting on a kind of apprenticeship in running the hotel as well as whistling. Yes, whistling, just like Ronnie Ronalde, who was famous on the music halls circuit at that time – his signature tune was '*If I was a blackbird, I'd whistle and sing.*' She became close friends with Joyce de Rhonda.

Eva had a strong Manx accent, a hybrid of Irish and Liverpudlian, as gentle a woman it would be hard to find, with a memory as sharp as a knife. She confirmed details about Cannon and the sisters de Rhonda which were also found in the MI5 file: "We got this letter with a terrific grand heading on it. There was almost a full page width of letters after his name. My mother actually wrote back and told them: 'I don't think this is the right hotel for you...' because they appeared to be so big... so grand. Too grand. But they still flew in and came and stayed with us."

73

As soon as they had arrived, the three attracted the attention of the authorities. Police established quite quickly that the two women accompanying Cannon were not from foreign climes, as some had assumed because of their strange accents. They were, as we know, sisters called Robson from north-east England, who had changed their names by deed poll. Geordie accents clearly were not widely recognised away from Tyneside back then, or else the sisters had consciously developed foreign accents to make themselves even more exotic than their names: Joyce and Rhonda de Rhonda, Dames of the Order of St Hubert. The combination of Whistling Eva and the de Rhonda sisters could barely have been more surreal.

When he first arrived, Cannon introduced his two assistants as his "wards" – he behaved like he was their employer and guardian. The women appeared to be three decades his junior. Eva Kane, who referred to Cannon as 'doctor', no definite article, emphasized many times – too many times? – that there was no question of any improper behaviour, despite the gossip on the island about what appeared to outsiders to be a bizarre ménage à trois: "There was nothing like that. Rhonda was his psychic assistant, Joyce, the younger, was the secretary and kept the business ticking over. Doctor was very much in charge."

My own grandmother, who lived and worked in Douglas all her life, had heard all the gossip, and referred to any women, be they patients or the sisters at the clinic, for whatever reason as 'those poor women'. As for Rhonda and Joyce, one was to leave and never speak to him again, the other spent the rest of her life with him.

Here was the puzzle of a divorced father of one who possessed a pathological desire to embroider his legitimate qualifications with lunatic claims. He seemed delighted that he looked older than he was, because he seemed to have felt it necessary to add twenty-seven years to his true age. There was never any doubt that this man who said he was the Kushog Yogi of Northern Tibet, a 'dun-yah kwair-kgh' like no other, would set tongues wagging, and alarm bells ringing amongst MI5 officers.

74

Eva Kane said while staying at the Falcon Cliff, first in 1939, and later in 1940, teetotal 'doctor' and the sisters spent a lot of time perched on high stools in the public bar, making friends, and very effective networkers they were too. Ellen and Leo had been ordered by then to keep the military personnel staying at their hotel separate from the civilian guests, but the Kanes were not inclined to follow orders from anyone. So Cannon probably got to know far more in the bar at the Falcon Cliff than the War Office would have approved of.

Wherever they went about their business, either at the hotel or in Douglas shopping, one thing was certain: the two Dames were sure to address the doctor, "Your Excellency!" in voices loud enough for all around to hear. He attracted the attention of the Manx press, but like all celebrities worth their salt, he refused to give an interview when requested. And so his air of mystique was nurtured.

Eva describes stories like they were yesterday, and underplays her celebrity status. When she was making a film on location in Douglas (remember: she was a music hall star), a request for an autograph was made by a little boy. Eva was in costume at that moment, and Dr Cannon and the sisters de Rhonda were watching the filming in their normal immaculate attire, including, in the hot sunshine, Cannon's standard frock coat and batwing collar. A little boy approached and asked Cannon for his autograph.

Doctor said to the boy: "Why do you want my autograph?" and the boy said: "I was told I could ask anyone in costume." Doctor, not well known for a sense of humour, was appalled.

75

Cannon and the ladies flew back to London after a failed week-long mission to find a property which matched Cannon's planned new image. But Ellen Kane kept searching the estate agents' offices, and after a few days she rang London to break the news they had been waiting for. She had found the perfect property.

Eva could still recall their delight: "Joyce flew straight back. She loved Ballamoar – and agreed to pay the princely sum of £8,000 for it. Nowadays you would shove a few noughts on the end of that."

Cannon as we now know had already filled his Welbeck Street

Clinic with Far Eastern artefacts and oil paintings gathered on his foreign journeys, the walls lined with books about black magic and the powers of the human mind. But the premises of this third clinic on the Isle of Man would be more exotic and impressive than either of the previous two.

Ballamoar stands at the end of a tree lined driveway worthy of any chateau in France. The house was built around the turn of the century, Victorian mock Gothic, with a low archway part masking a heavy mock Tudor front door which opens into an oak-panelled, galleried hallway with a vast fireplace. It was the perfect location for a huge oil painting of himself in Masonic regalia which hung there when Cannon was in residence, looking down on visitors to his castle. How had he come to have a portrait painted by Arthur Pan, a distinguished Hungarian artist, whose paintings of Churchill and the Queen are well-known?

When it came to the day Dr Cannon and the ladies moved in, it was memorable for the removal men, one of whom reminisced on Manx Radio many years later: "There was a tremendous amount of antiques. He had all kinds of strange equipment. He had one machine – massive it was – it just vibrated your whole body. I had never seen anything like it. Two Chinese statues stood over eight foot high. They were stood outside the building at the main doorway, like they were on guard."

Eva's memory was just as clear, but she could not quite remember my mother's family. My grandfather, another tax exile, found the Kanes useful guides when he took his family to stay in the Falcon Cliff Hotel in 1949. My mother has a photograph of her mother with Two Ton Tessie O'Shea and George Elrick, the Terry Wogan of his day, on the terrace.

76

Eva could clearly remember George Drummond, who stayed at the Falcon Cliff at the same time as Cannon and his dames. The reason for his move to the Isle of Man at the start of the war was never spelled out to the Kanes, they did not ask the 'big man' the reason for his move. Drummond arrived with Eve, one of his four daughters from his first marriage, along with a young woman who was initially presented as Eve's friend. Falcon Cliff had a number of sizeable rooms with fantastic views of Douglas Bay. Eva Kane recalled certain shenanigans about who was staying in which bedroom.

"My mother allotted the best room to George Drummond as he was 'The Big Man'. His daughter and (who we thought was) her friend got very nice rooms too. We found out later on that Eve's 'friend' stayed in George Drummond's room." She turned out to be the woman that he later married: Miss Honora Myrtle Spiller, a good deal younger than he was, the daughter of a wealthy family living in Ireland.

Aside from noticing that she ended up in the old man's bed, the Kanes had not the faintest idea of the intrigue and scandal swirling around the Drummonds. George fathered eight children in all. To avoid the ignominy of a Manx birth in exile, King George VI arranged for Honora to give birth to Honora and George's first child at Windsor Castle in 1943. What's more, despite Drummond's clear Nazi sympathies, the King even agreed to be George Albert Harley Drummond's godfather.

Meantime back on the island, his daughter, Eve Drummond, described by MI5 as "a daughter of the famous banking family, patient of Cannon, a bright young thing who drank too much and a

Nazi sympathiser", got to know Eva and the sisters de Rhonda quite well. She was banned from drinking with military men on the island as she was prone to argue with them that the war was 'futile'.

Both Drummond and Cannon (if he needed one) had keep-out-of-internment-camp cards: the lurid detail of their behind the scenes accounts of the abdication. Nothing I have seen hints at blackmail, but it is worth considering. Drummond was banker to the royals; Cannon could be described as 'Britain's Rasputin'. The Times had already had some knowledge of the story.

77

Before the arrival of the internees, there was deep concern on the Isle of Man. As the declaration of war in September 1939 turned into what was known as the Phoney War (when anticipated battles did not happen), alarm spread amongst hoteliers. All of a sudden, the holidaymakers had disappeared. The distant war had taken away their livelihoods. There were no tourists to eat the famous Manx ice cream or drink pints of Okells bitter; no more parcels of Manx kippers in the ferry holds. A very bureaucratic Ministry of Food in London saw to that.

Travelling to Liverpool had become a nightmare of form-filling and identity cards. Husbands and fathers went to join the forces. The island's lifeline steamers were requisitioned as quickly as the boarding houses. The Steam Packet Company had to supply men as well as boats to fight Hitler. Where there had been sixteen daily ferry sailings to British ports, suddenly there were only six.

Guest house landladies were vocal about their concerns. With so many men gone, and no tourists, how would they feed their families?

A promise of payments to look after child evacuees never materialised. An emergency meeting of the Boarding House and Apartment Association agreed the following advert should be placed in the London newspapers:

Isle of Man.
A Really Permanent Place of Security
Safe accommodation to suit all pockets
Very reasonable terms. Home Farm produce
Regular mail boat services to and from Liverpool

It was a flop, it did not generate enough business to pay for itself, and the Manx trod water for a while. But then things speeded up: more and more hotels were requisitioned as billets for the officers who were setting up training camps. Ellen Kane decided not to put up with the ridiculous low rentals offered. She took herself along to complain to the military authorities and moved out of the Falcon Cliff to a boarding house as a protest. Lucky that her husband Leo Kane was onto a really good thing – driving up north every day to supervise the building work at Ballamoar.

Then, in the spring of 1940, the Phoney War really did come to an end. The Nazi war machine goose-stepped across northern Europe, and Churchill stepped up the indiscriminate arrests not only of foreign aliens, even those who simply had a German surname, but also Blackshirts.

"Collar the lot!" he famously declared. Pro-Nazi and left wing or non-political Germans and Italians were banged up willy nilly with Jews and British fascists. The knock on the door meant the removal of many people, many very bewildered because they had been chased out of Europe and their only offence was their nationality.

The world famous Amadeus String Quartet originally came together in the Isle of Man internment camp in Hutchinson Square in Douglas, the island's capital. The random round-up had included violinists Norbert Brainin, Siegmund Nissel and Peter Schidlof, all of them driven out of Vienna after Hitler's Anschluss of 1938 because they were Jewish. Brainin was released after a few months, but Schidlof remained in the camp, where he met Nissel. It took a long time for the British security services to filter out the real fascist troublemakers and street fighters and send them down the road to the Peveril Camp in Peel.

Canada and Australia offered to take these aliens 'away from temptation', and more than ten thousand were shipped off to Canada. But U-boat attacks made this impractical – five hundred people were lost when a liner was torpedoed on the way to Australia. So the Cabinet decided the Isle of Man was much more convenient, making use of those boarding houses not used by the military. And in later years, it was Dr Cannon who vetted many of them. It was some of these prisoners who provided Gastor with so much information.

78

The first prison camp was on the Mooragh Promenade in Ramsey. Initially, thirty houses were requisitioned. Later, whole stretches of promenade and scores of hotels and guest houses in Ramsey and Douglas had to be vacated immediately; personal furniture was jammed into tea chests, valued and recorded and stacked in store in church halls. Landladies and their families had to move in with friends and family who lived in smaller houses in the countryside. Beds were suddenly very scarce and sold at a premium, and then adverts began to appear for employment of all kinds – guards, cooks, drivers. Tenders were put out for huge quantities of milk, bread, meat, potatoes jam and sugar.

By the end of May 1940, the early stage of the Mooragh Camp was ready to take hundreds of high security risk prisoners. Guarded by a hundred and fifty troops, on the first day after the Dunkirk evacuations, 823 men arrived in Ramsey within twenty four hours.

Connery Chappell, in his book The Island of Barbed Wire, described the first arrivals: "The youngest were schoolboys in shorts; only a few appeared to be anywhere near the age limit of sixty. They came ashore on Ramsey's iron pier, carrying suitcases, small hand luggage, parcels or even bundles on their backs. Once off the ships they were allowed to put heavier baggage on the trolleys and a number of men pushed their loads to the ends of the pier. One internee was holding his portable typewriter, the other his fishing rod."

In a comparatively short space of time, the population was militarised. The island was remote, too far from the Luftwaffe to be bombed and had plenty of accommodation. New training bases for personnel for the Air Arm of the Navy and two RAF bases were built and expanded in the north of the island. One of these, at Jurby, was right next to Ballamoar Castle.

By mid-July, 8,500 men were interned on the island and then the whole of the southern town of Port Erin was surrounded with barbed wire and turned over to 3,500 women internees. Every week it seemed a new development had to be dealt with. At the Esplanade Café, my grandmother, Caroline Stowell, did a roaring trade. Conscripts loved her chips and flirted with her daughters.

Each boat from Liverpool brought with it a new batch of people to absorb: some prisoners, some military staff; some were wounded, recuperating post-Dunkirk – and taken to Falcon Cliff – as by June that year it had been turned into a military hospital. Depending on rank, others were taken to Ballamoar Castle for the Cannon treatment.

From the authorities' point of view, the Isle of Man Clinic for Nervous Disorders was a bizarre set-up run by an eccentric doctor who was treating selected senior members of the military with exotic hypnotic therapies while enjoying the most lavish lifestyle on the island. From the point of view of people who lived locally, there were great suspicions.

Indeed, one man describing himself as a 'loyal subject' wrote to the chief constable of the island: "There are many people in the north of the island who are wondering why a man of pronounced Nazi views is allowed to live at Ballamoar near Jurby airport. It is stated that he has written a book which is pro-Nazi… When our country has been betrayed it will be too late to take steps. Please do it now."

79

It had taken almost a year to set up Dr Cannon's clinic. Spending a lot of time in London on 'special projects', throughout the rest of 1939 and the start of 1940, Cannon had left the sisters de Rhonda in charge, the Kane family doing much of the actual work to transform Ballamoar Castle into a clinic totally unique in the whole of Europe, occupied or otherwise, for many reasons, including the fact that it was also getting a sewage plant as well as an electricity generator all of its own. Probably no other building in the world could rival Ballamoar for what went on there. And what is more, despite the suspicions swirling around him, the owner was seen to be making money hand over fist from mystical, occult-style goings-on, from yoga to spiritualist contacts beyond the grave, to lessons in telepathy in the grand gardens.

But Cannon's world did not just spring up on its own. Mr Kane had had to see to building those wooden treatment rooms, or 'therapy sheds', at the rear of the premises. Weird and wonderful medical and scientific machinery had to be installed; the generator had to be built and get working for fear the local power supplies fail. Walls and ceilings were to be painted black in some rooms in the house and in all of the treatment rooms at the rear, and then the silver stars added. Not so easy given the wartime rationing conditions. But the sisters de Rhonda, the Kanes and Dr Cannon pulled all that suspicious work off against all odds and right next door to an RAF aerodrome. It had not gone unnoticed however.

80

As the letter from the 'loyal subject' shows, it had not taken long for lots of dots to be joined up amongst the Manx, especially when Cannon's talk of 'the power of one man to lead millions' and 'masters of destiny' was overheard in pubs and hotels and then read in his books. His close relationship with another bizarre threesome, the Drummonds, attracted attention too. They went around calling the war 'futile' – and only fascists said such things.

So, as far as the outside world was concerned, Cannon was sympathetic to the Germans, and had lots of bizarre electrical machinery in a 'castle' isolated in the north of the island, not far from key shipping lanes where predatory U-boats were on the prowl. Could his machinery be used to communicate with them? Was it interfering with RAF Jurby's radio communications at the aerodrome next door? Cannon told everyone that the house stood in part of the British Isles uniquely placed for cross-over international radio communications.

81

But there were royal egos involved in the question of how to deal with the Cannon affair. The island's governor, Earl Granville, outraged that the girls called Cannon 'Your Excellency' – "There's only one Excellency on this island, and it's me!" – ordered the island's chief constable to investigate The Clinic. As the then Queen Mother's brother-in-law, Lord Granville may well have known about Cannon's past encounters with the very temporary King Edward VIII. Was it despite, or because of that, he never held back from expressing his wish to have him chased off the island?

Chief constable Major John Young knew Cannon was well-connected, but to Berlin as well? Like Earl Granville, Young definitely had his suspicions, and he lost no time in ordering an investigation to safeguard not only King and Country, but also his lordship's right to be the only one on the Isle of Man who could rightfully have himself referred to as 'His Excellency'. In any case, the Metropolitan Police in London and MI5 in Whitehall were already making inquiries and asking questions.

Cannon was a man with a past which only a handful knew about. The spy chiefs thought they knew him, understood him, but doubt had begun to creep in the more his connections with Nazis became known. Was there something else they did not know about? The question on the island became: who was it who was so powerful to be able to look after him so well? Had he made contact with Nazi Germany well before the war?

Servant of London, as he will have seen himself, Major Young could only see a fog of rumour and supposition. But faced with a monolithic secret service bureaucracy, in the early days of his Cannon watch he felt he had better get his act together and see what was what.

82

Major Young had set up the Manx CID only two years before war broke out. He was resentful his new systems were being over-ruled because of the invasion of military security personnel. MI5 had been expanded very quickly and not very effectively by Whitehall– some were rank amateurs and posh with it. They thought a public school education and an upper class twang meant they could waltz in to the

Isle of Man and take over from and routinely patronize 'locals'. Major Young would never have said as much, his deference could always be relied on – he had not got to be chief constable without due deference. He could not let his resentment about the new chaps on the block cloud his judgment. This weirdo doctor had to be checked out – there could be no spying revelations on his watch.

So who would lead Operation Cannon? One of his crack inspectors of many years' experience was known to be cool-headed and not ruffled by pressures of hierarchy. When it came to assessing whether Cannon was spy or conman, he was the man for the job.

Inspector William Kneen was a Manxman of few words. But when he did speak his mind, it could be with devastating effect. He had no hang-ups to hold him back about highlighting the inadequacies of the posh boys from 'across'.

An inspector with years of experience, a wily fox. When told of his latest operation, he suspected he would enjoy sparring mind games with Dr Cannon. The Fascists ended up being just a few miles down the road from Ballamoar and one of the scenarios Kneen considered was that any internee could be a pathway of communication between Cannon and the enemy.

Another scenario revealed by the MI5 documents was that Cannon was allegedly, rather fantastically, communicating with U-boats off the northern tip of the island. In reality, the numbers of permutations were endless – any inquiry had to have focus.

Inspector Kneen had most of his time taken up policing the Fascists interned at Peveril Camp – the prisoners who would ironically get to know Dr Cannon very well. An audacious and initially successful escape plot would come to implicate Dr Cannon and for some weeks both the prisoners and the doctor ended up dominating all the Inspector's waking hours. Prisoners had successfully dug a long, complex tunnel worthy of any Great Escape scenario. Two escaped and stole a boat; heading for Ireland barely a mile or two from the Manx coast, they were subsequently captured. A riot followed at Peel camp and it was a while before order was restored amongst the fascists. Right at the start of what was to become a protracted crisis, police had been immediately dispatched to Ballamoar to question Cannon directly, such were the suspicions that had built up around him.

But at the start of the Cannon inquiry in July 1940, Major Young was a master of discretion. He kick started Operation Cannon by writing to the Postmaster in Douglas: "Sir, I venture to enquire whether I can enlist your assistance in a matter directly affecting security control in this island. I refer to one known as Dr Alexander Cannon... in whom for the reason I have mentioned above, I am deeply interested and in whose 'business' it is considered vital to keep in close, but secret, contact.

"To enable me to ensure this, I would be grateful for your co-operation in so far as it lies within your jurisdiction in obtaining from today a copy of all telegrams arriving at and dispatched from Ballamoar and similarly, all telephonic communications to and from Dr Cannon's residence and the mainland. It is perhaps needless for me to say that should my request receive favourable consideration, the greatest secrecy would be observed throughout."

Another inquiry had already been made of the Metropolitan police in London as to whether he had a licence to have a radio, and the answer came back that he had never had relevant clearance, though he was strongly rumoured to have a radio. So finally there was a concrete reason for searching Ballamoar. Inspector Kneen wasted no time in executing a search warrant on 9th July 1940 at 15.20 hours.

83

The inspector sat up till the early hours writing his report that same night, making careful use to objectify his observations with 'appeared': "Dr Cannon appeared to be very anxious to give us every assistance… He appeared to be very frank and open about everything; he informed us that there were twelve patients staying with him. He showed us a list of appointments. He told us he made his own gramophone records and allowed us to hear one: a record of Dr Cannon's voice dictating an auto-suggestive mantra aimed at encouraging a sick individual to believe in the beauty of his body and soul, and that he was getting younger and better as the days passed."

They had found nothing thus far which could be described as *definitely* suspicious, whilst a lot of what they found *could* have been suspicious. The Inspector's first conclusion: Cannon was merely an eccentric. In this first official foray into Cannon's world, he described his clinical practices for the treatment of nervous disorders – electrical apparatus and other "highly technical appliances" (his words) which had been imported from London. There was a Wimshurst machine – two spinning wheels two foot six inches in diameter which generated huge sparks of electricity. There were violet and infra-red light treatment units, and high-frequency vibration machinery. This was the apparatus which some contested interfered with the wireless telegraphic apparatus at the Jurby airfield. Not only that – had he been making 'illicit' wireless transmissions to an enemy?

"There was a gramophone in one of the consulting rooms amongst a lot of other electrical apparatus… and two beds in each room with blankets and pillows. He told me the patient receives electrical treatment whilst lying in or on the bed and at the same time listening to Dr Cannon's record. It was just the kind of treatment which might affect the sick or weak mind, but to me it just seemed like a kind of cheap quackery.

"He mentioned he knows there are rumours about him, that he had heard it even suggested that he was a German; he had considered putting a notice in the press giving his history and warning persons against reporting such rumours. From what I saw at Ballamoar I am reluctant to believe that Dr Cannon is in any way interested in illicit wireless communications.

"He is strange; his manner, speech and bearing hardly that of a professional man, whilst his two women secretaries are the type of women usually found behind the bar in a hotel smoke room. They do not conduct themselves as employees but rather as if they were part and parcel of Dr Cannon himself."

84

Each Cannon memo arriving on the Major's desk was more worrying than the previous one. For example, one from Sergeants Kay and Duncalf of the RAF Service Security Police concerned alleged security breaches at a very important RAF station at Bride, a couple of miles north west of Ballamoar. It was used for Direction Finding Signals for RAF aircraft.

This station was part of the Chain Home system which could determine distance and direction of incoming aircraft formations and was linked to two other radar stations on the island: one at Dalby near Peel, and one at Scarlett, near Castletown, and from there to the Lancashire coast. Four months before Sergeants Kay and Metcalf wrote their memo, an off-shoot of 9 Group Fighter Command, had moved to RAF Jurby, the airfield over the fence from Ballamoar, a site selected for its location in relation to Liverpool, Belfast and Glasgow. Kay and Metcalfe were charged with the task of the security at the base where personnel felt relaxed about the eccentric Dr Cannon, who allowed them to park aircraft under the camouflage of his trees on the edge of the Ballamoar estate.

The RAF had come to the island because the Luftwaffe had begun to bomb the industrial cities of northern England, previously beyond their range. Now the Germans were striking from airfields in occupied northern France. This bombing of the north west of England began in October 1940, so the Isle of Man provided an ideal location for 9 Group.

Under these new pressures, the new wing of Ramsey Grammar School, just down the road from Ballamoar, was commissioned as Control Centre and was hastily prepared before the arrival of the new fighters at Jurby, next door to Ballamoar. The sergeants reveal details of an 'alarming' incident and the identity of one of the high-ranking military men under the influence of Dr Cannon and who had access to highly significant battle plans.

Sergeant Kay was upset: "On one occasion the transmissions from Bride suffered some interference and F/O Ligertwood states that he believes the interference to have been caused by Dr Cannon's apparatus. Again on the night of the 12/3/41 during an alert, the transmissions from the south of the Isle of Man were interfered with. Enemy aircraft appear to circle off the Point of Ayre, and it is possible that they may be receiving messages or bearings from Ballamoar. F/O Ligertwood said that he had tried to detect the wireless transmissions but without success and suggested that some inaudible signal such as television may have been employed.

"There are parallel roads, one on either side of the RAF Bride station and about four months ago, F/O Ligertwood was involved in a slight collision with a car whose occupants included Dr Cannon, a man who claims to be Admiral Davies, and two women of foreign appearance."

Admiral Davies was a key figure in the North Atlantic convoys on which Britain's war effort so depended, given the stranglehold German u-boats had on vital Atlantic supply lines. Ligertwood later learned that another car had been stopped on the other side road and only one of the occupants had an identity card. He suggests that the two cars may have been involved in taking a bearing to discover the exact location of an RAF transmitter, and that seamen landing on the island may give away movements of shipping, and that these details find their way via the alien women at Ballamoar to be transmitted 'elsewhere'. The account ends with a remark about official inertia to do anything about Cannon, something which is a significant feature of the story of Dr Cannon: "F/O Ligertwood has reported the matter to various officers of 60 Group, Fighter Command, but has seen no results yet. On another occasion, the local police were trying to locate a car from which it was suspected pictures of a naval camp were being taken. Our informant feels certain Dr Cannon was in the car. We also heard that he sometimes obtains permission to fly in RAF planes to the mainland."

Failure to have identity cards was without doubt a reason for justifiable suspicion. Foreign appearance less so. But this final comment about Cannon flying in and out of the Isle of Man in RAF aircraft turned out to be absolutely true. But from whom was he getting permission to fly in and out like he was someone of great importance? Perhaps he was someone significant. Had he stuck two of his fat fingers up at gob-smacked agents who gawped each time his plane took off from RAF Jurby, it would have been entirely fitting.

85

Cannon sat tight for a number of months while inquiry after inquiry flew back and forth from MI5 in London, Oxford and the Isle of Man. He was aware of what was going on but most probably knew nothing of a key development, one which triggered a request from the War Office for a full report on him: a letter written on April 12th, and addressed to "Chief Intelligence Department, Whitehall."

Margot H. Johnson, of Albany Street in Douglas wrote: "I know this person intimately... I cannot mention any names as this letter may fall into hands other than your own. I know things which no-one else knows as I have had his confidence for some time past. At the expense of appearing melodramatic I say that no time should be lost if the outcome of this war is to be what we are all fighting for. Full inquiries and investigation should be made as I am sure you will agree what I am able to tell you. But every day matters if what I suspect is true."

Margot Johnson advised against landing planes at Jurby aerodrome as: "the person concerned has ways and means of finding out many things in the neighbourhood. Again I am perfectly certain my own life would be in danger if he were to discover that I had 'betrayed' him. I am very serious in this matter and it had to be almost a certainty before I decided to take this step."

New Scotland Yard Commissioner Sir Norman Kendal wrote to Major Young. Sir Norman wanted to know if there were any more developments about Cannon, known to be "living extravagantly with curious lady friends" and using fraudulent titles such as "Knight Commander of the Order of Asia…which if it exists at all it is the creation of some mountebank who sells it to other mountebanks." And the Margot Johnson letter had reinforced deeply-held suspicions.

86

Inspector Kneen's back was up. He was not going to stand for any nonsense from London about the many rumours of espionage; he had identified Cannon's love of "creating an air of mystery around himself"; the weirdness of the sisters de Rhonda deferentially addressing Cannon as 'Your Excellency' in public places; and the fact that every intelligence officer as soon as he arrived on the island had picked up and probably embroidered the gossip.

Another report arrived containing accusations from the RAF Service Security Police. Inspector Kneen was beside himself: "…after 28 years' service it is the most highly coloured report I have read". The warrant to search for a wireless transmitter had proved to be fruitless. So what more could he do?

Major Young wrote to Sir Norman to back up his Inspector: "The relatively abortive results from our inquiries – you asked him to find evidence of illegal radio transmissions, and he found none – are caused by Dr Cannon's aptitude for the stage-management of every situation. Whilst his conduct is doubtless open to question, I agree with my inspector's summary: he is a strange fish, but no piranha."

87

*For a specialist in mental diseases not to be conventional
is to some an unpardonable crime*

Alexander Cannon

Major Young and Inspector Kneen were not on their own when it came to pressure to sort Cannon: Agent Sykes of MI5 in Oxford was getting ear ache too from the complex security network over on the Isle of Man, and that was some weeks even before the letter from Margot Johnson which raised sinister possibilities. A letter landed in Sykes' intray from Lord Greenway, the Commander of the Onchan camp, dated 9th March 1941.

In it he stated he and the other titled camp commandants (they all seemed to be barons, lords or sirs) were not very satisfied with the position as regards Cannon who they suspected was a spy. Lord Greenway had brought the matter to the attention of the local authorities but got no response. Perhaps someone should cut through these bureaucractic barriers and infiltrate the clinic to see what the hell was going on once and for all?

Not for the first time, Cannon's clinic was to be targeted, and Agent Sykes was clever in his selection of infiltrator. In fact the choice was inadvertently determined by Lord Greenway himself. She was someone who had been over to the island to speak at an event he had organized.

MI5's unofficial agent was Dr Doris Odlum, a formidable woman, a member of the British Medical Association's psychiatric committee and an ex-suffragette who had, like Cannon, got her medical education after service in the First World War. She studied classics at Oxford and then medicine. She had worked for the same London County Mental Health Service as Cannon – the Service which had sacked him eight years before. So she was to be despatched by a low-ranking MI5 officer into Ballamoar. It was clear that whilst Kneen was certain Cannon was not a spy, Sykes was still very suspicious.

The clinic's proximity to a Bomber Command aerodrome was just one aspect of her investigation as he had such easy access to military top brass. Cannon was also said to be "hail-fellow-well-met" with workmen, pilots, and admirals, something which alarmed Major d'Eggville, MI5's man in charge in Douglas. Lord Greenway wrote: "He evidently gets information about the movements at Jurby. He also gets a lot of officers as patients but it is impossible to ascertain whether they are stationed at Jurby or are officers who come over from the mainland for treatment for battle fatigue."

For Odlum, the mission was no hardship, she knew exactly what to do: appeal to his vanity. She told him she had heard he was having some success in working with shell-shocked and mentally disturbed combatants, a cornerstone of any psychiatrist's work for a large part of the 20th century. She believed she could learn much from observing his methods, she would 'learn from a master'.

So she booked in for a few days as a guest at the clinic. The fact that Odlum was on the British Medical Association's psychiatric committee was testament in itself of the suspicions swirling around Cannon. She knew how to establish facts about Cannon, and then find a definitive answer to the big question about him flying around the island.

She was taken aback by the excellent food and wine provided, unheard of in food-rationed Britain. She was one of the very few people to tease out of him the fact that he had a wife and a child. She was deeply unimpressed with security arrangements at the clinic given the suspicions against the government's hypnotist-in-chief – if that was what he was.

Agent Sykes wrote a report after a debriefing session at Doctor Odlum's practice in Bournemouth in March 1941. "Dr Odlum... thinks he might use hypnotic methods to get information out of his patients. We discussed whether it is possible to do so against his or her will. Some years ago it was the medical opinion that this was not possible, but Dr Odlum says the medical men are not so sure nowadays; they know too little about hypnotism to form a judgement.

"But in answer to my question, Dr Odlum said that, making full use of the theatrical effects such as the black walls and star spangled ceilings etc with music and incense, it might be that the patient would part with information, if in a fit state of mind, even before Cannon applied the fluence."

She reported suspicions against him heightened when a row of trees which obscured the view from the house to the RAF Jurby airfield had been chopped down by order of the doctor, despite the fact that they acted as a shield against the violent north wind on that exposed Manx coast.

She ascertained he definitely trained as a doctor in Leeds, and was a Master of Arts at Cambridge. The PhD after his name she strangely took as evidence of studying at a German-speaking university. "Also, he has Harley Street rooms which he does not use now he has set up in the Isle of Man. In the Mental Hospital service (sic) Cannon was regarded as a queer fish because he talked continually of the efficacy of electrical healing methods such as etheric waves, yoga vibrations etc."

She tracked down *The Invisible Influence,* noting his advocacy of diagnosis and healing by hypnotism, vibrations and that his London County Hospital employers, for whom she also worked at that time, considered that the publication of this book was incompatible with the position that he held, and therefore dismissed him. After this time, he was wont to hire a London hotel room on a Sunday afternoon and hold séances.

Delving into the history of his career, Dr Odlum discovered that he sued the health authority in London over the dismissal, and won his job back, although he was no longer interested in it. There comes an eighteen month gap in his life at this point, at least as far as the medical directory is concerned, with no evidence that he practised his profession in any way. Where Cannon disappeared to, no-one knows. As we know, it was after this gap in his career that he set up the lucrative clinic in London. But Dr Odlum could not explain the source of wealth which allowed him to do that, given his previous low wages at Colney Hatch Mental Hospital.

Sykes wrote: "Colney Hatch is not the type of appointment any ambitious medical man would take. The commencing salary is about £300 a year, rising by small increments to £500 or £600 a year with a pension on retiring. This is the sort of job which would attract mediocrity anxious for safety first whereas his Harley Street rooms were furnished exotically with black walls and star-spangled ceilings so that evidently he was out to attract the credulous type of patient in search of exotic healing methods."

And then Sykes describes the fairground roles played by the sisters de Rhonda: "He diagnoses by means of two mediums who he puts into hypnotic trances. But when invited to demonstrate his methods… he came a very sad cropper. His claims to be able to diagnose both neurological and organic diseases by these methods fail in both directions."

Dr Odlum scorned his curious claims to titles: "He has no British titles which would warrant him being sometimes styled Sir Alexander Cannon but does hold the title of Commandatore Cavaliere in Italy which he claims is equivalent to a Baronetcy.

"True – it is a title, but a cheap one, ranking far below that of a British knighthood."

Odlum then takes the reader on a tour of the Manx mansion: sixteen rooms expressly designed to take up to ten visiting patients at a time at a charge of three guineas per treatment. He insists on each patient receiving a minimum of seven treatments, but Dr Odlum could not work out the charges for board and lodgings. And she noted that whatever happens beyond the house in terms of power cuts – storm damage is common on the island – he had his own private electricity supply so patients' comfort could always be assured (thanks to Leo kane). Yet more reason, said Agent Sykes, to wonder just who was backing him, and what he was preparing for. He built numerous out-houses for the purpose of his scientific experiments.

"He brought over expensive electrical equipment at a time when no-one was allowed to bring such items to the Isle of Man and many people are curious as to the way in which he contrived to get permission. Obviously he has some pull somewhere and one wonders in which direction to look for it, but perhaps that might be a separate line of investigation."

Perhaps the 'pull' lay with the bankers and aristocrats on his list of patients, or perhaps the 'pull' lay at the very top of Admiralty and MI5?

Agent Sykes listed patients who had been treated and cites their broader connections within the smart set... "Miss Eve Drummond, a daughter of the famous banking family, was formerly his patient. She is said to be a bright young thing who drinks too much. Miss Drummond is now on the Isle of Man. The Drummonds are said to be Nazi sympathizers and friendly with some foreigners of the name Huntziger who are unaccountably allowed to be at large in the IoM where residence is normally forbidden to all aliens (except those behind barbed wire). The Drummonds are also friendly with Sir Mark Lidgett and Montagu Norman..."

Norman had been the Governor of the Bank of England and hugely important on the political scene, especially when it came to acting as a conduit between Hitler and the City of London financiers.

There were twelve persons staying at the clinic while Dr. Odlum was there – twelve men and nine women. Dr. Odlum sat next to a Mrs Davies who had with her a son – an RAF officer – and a daughter. Two of this trio might be in a position to give Cannon information likely to be of use to the enemy, if he could extract it from them.

Sykes continued: "He is a hypnotist himself but in answer to Dr Odlum's question, said that he no longer hypnotizes patients himself because this would make him too deeply involved in their minds. The elder de Rhonda acts as his hostess. She struck Dr Odlum as exceedingly clever but reserved and rather sinister, probably unscrupulous and a stronger personality than Cannon himself. The younger sister (Joyce) acts as his secretary, describing her as queer, rabbitty and rather unstable.

"As for Cannon's use of electrotherapy equipment: this apparatus is not permitted nowadays as it could easily be converted into a transmitter and it is clear the man knows enough about electricity to make a transmitter set.. and in fact has already done so since Lord Greenway and Commander Mounthays (Internment Camp Commanders) and the Governor of the Isle of Man (Lord Granville) maintain that wireless messages in code were detected coming from his house."

Rather tellingly, Dr Odlum also noticed official inertia when it came to Dr Cannon: "Dr Odlum commented that no-one had followed up these claims, as information sent to the police 'never led to any results'. So the only hope for any action was to communicate the facts to MI5 And the facts are: He is a bounder and a liar!"

In conclusion: "Wealthy, fashionable patients do not like to make long and difficult journeys for their treatment. Dr Odlum said from her own experience it would be the last place such a doctor would hit upon. She could have understood it if he had set himself up in the Lake District which is crowded with wealthy people who have left London to get away from the bombing… But the trip to the IoM with the enforced break in the journey at frequently-bombed Liverpool, plus the questions put by the authorities to intending travellers, plus a rough sea passage... these are not circumstances which would improve the conditions of his type of patient."

The report, put together by Agent Sykes and Doris Odlum, provided some of the most damning evidence against Dr Cannon. It was written up, stamped 'TOP SECRET' and sent to P.O.Box 500 or 'Snuffbox' – but it had little impact. Had they been on the island, they would only have seen that Cannon continued as before: two fingers up to everyone.

88

And yet, perhaps there really were reasons that this Dr 'Sir' Alexander Cannon should have been rigorously questioned. The possibility that Cannon was a German agent can never really be discounted. If he was a traitor, the Germans will have been delighted with him given the calibre of patient he had coming through his doors, their heads jam-packed with secret battle plans.

And he appeared to engender blind faith amongst his patients, another reason for him to be the perfect agent. One regular visitor, aside from many other top drawer military chiefs, would never hear a word said against the doctor and was on board enough to get his wife to become a Ballamoar regular too. The rear admiral referred to by the RAF police, Admiral Davies, had retired in 1926 but returned to serve as the Commodore of the Convoys across the Atlantic, co-ordinating auxiliary and merchant ships which were keeping Britain afloat with supplies from America.

Without convoy defence, Britain would have gone under given the dreadful toll exacted by U-boats. The discovery of Enigma code machines was also crucial to breaking Germany's Atlantic U-boat, something to which Dr Cannon would later claim a direct contribution.

Admiral Davies was based at the Combined Operations headquarters and the headquarters of the RAF's No.15 Group coastal command in Liverpool. Incredibly, he was just one of a number of admirals, commanders and the titled baronets coming through Cannon's doors.

There could have been no place better than Ballamoar Castle for a stressed, hauled-out-of-retirement admiral with an historic military battle on his hands – and a demanding wife to boot who had health issues. From the files it emerged that he sometimes stayed at Liverpool's famous Adelphi Hotel – and tended to be a little bit absent-minded.

On one occasion, he left a bunch of letters and papers in his room, a mishap which would highlight the bizarrely relaxed attitude towards Cannon shown by those at the very top of the security service tree compared to those lower down.

Once Admiral Davies had discovered he had left them behind, the Manx CID intercepted a telegram from him on the island to the hotel in Liverpool: "Priority: Manager, Adelphi Hotel, Liverpool. Letters etc left room 603, please forward Ballamoar, Ramsey, Isle of Man."

MI5's Director General Sir David Petrie was informed immediately. He was told in a letter from CID in Douglas and Special Branch in Liverpool that the paperwork had been returned by registered post. Special Branch's Sergeant Jones added that inquiries had been made, and a senior intelligence officer within the Navy claimed Davies lived at Ballamoar Castle. Alarm was expressed that Davies could be telling Cannon anything, and who knows what the doctor was getting up to.

Sir David's laid-back response was that "if Dr Cannon is dangerous, *the Admiral should be informed in case he confides in him.*" And no further communication from him appears in the file. Either any follow-up was removed, or he decided Dr Cannon was playing games and posed no threat.

All these security people – all these doubts – was he playing games in the middle of a war or was he in fact a spy? And there in black and white was an order from the top that 'the Admiral should be careful.' And so Cannon managed to continue being a potential 'information leak' to the Germans for many more months, and even the most powerful figures did not seem bothered. He was, one could argue, being protected by Petrie. But why?

89

More evidence of protection from on high came in July 1941 when he came a cropper professionally and ethically. He had sent a sick note to a long-standing patient in England – a paid full-time air raid warden, Herbert Latreille of Beckenham in Kent - to say he should be allowed time off work for no less than three weeks. "To not allow this would be criminal".

The *News Chronicle* reported that Cannon had told Latreille's bosses he had diagnosed his problems telepathically. The GMC found a complaint against Cannon for fraud proven, but the committee hearing the case was prepared to believe that Cannon had signed the certificates "not from any perversity or desire to falsify, but from a mistaken view of his duties and an error of judgment." Such a case today would result in indignant headlines.

More importantly, the General Medical Council had missed a chance to sort out Cannon once and for all. Internally, London police chief Sir Norman Kendal (a security service outsider) had flagged up the case in advance, hoping someone in authority would ensure he was finally struck off. But that is exactly what did not happen, despite it being a clearly open and shut case. A serial-offender doctor who had been sacked before and who was said to be a 'Black Magic master' was allowed to stay practising as a doctor despite having claimed to diagnose a patient telepathically.

Inspector Kneen was perplexed by the goings-on but unsurprised.

He, not Major Young, reported back to Sir Norman Kendal that while he had an open mind about the doctor – he would keep an eye on him – he was however suspicious of his association with two other men: one, Captain John Ernest Dudley Scott, the other, Captain George Drummond, who attracted attention for very different reasons. It was those two who really caught Kneen's eye, he told Sir Norman.

Both were protected by their cut glass class and accents and friends in high places. Both did come under closer scrutiny for their suspicious behaviour, and their dismissive attitudes to authority drew Cannon into their danger zones, making the doctor finally vulnerable in ways he may not have otherwise been.

90

Aided by the power of darkness telepathy can be practised even on those between whom there is no real conscious affinity

Alexander Cannon

Cannon's MI5 file shows how admirals and RAF officers bought into Dr Cannon's thinking in a big way, despite gossip and rumour that he was a Nazi agent, or at the very least a sympathiser.

The comment from Agent Sykes and MI5's clinic infiltrator Dr Odlum that Cannon was protected by someone with 'pull' was telling. So who was tugging the strings and protecting him from the lower ranks, and more importantly why was that happening? Was he involved with a particular project too secret for officers to know about, and which meant regularly flying to bases in England? Some, including John Gastor, claimed Cannon's influence went right to the top and went as far as Downing Street.

91

Amongst the Cannon converts who were commanders in the military – the Ballamoarians – there was, believe it or not, excited talk of using telepathy as a desperately needed weapon against the U-boats. The Battle of the Atlantic meant the Germans were increasing their stranglehold on the UK's transatlantic supplies. There was gossip amongst clinic regulars that Dr Cannon was in the vanguard of developing a telepathic method that could be deployed against submarines.

Moreover, telepathy could be used to deliver mind control *Manchurian Candidate*-style missions (dormant or sleeper mind-controlled agent goes on assassination operation), so Cannon's theories went, as spelt out in *The Invisible Influence*. Joyce de Rhonda was involved, and a couple of other names were mentioned.

One of those names was John Ernest Dudley Scott, a young aristocrat with mental health problems who stayed for long spells at Cannon's clinic. Banned from driving for five years for a string of driving offences, Scott mystified and infuriated security officers both on the island and in England with his complete disregard for their authority.

Scott already had the support of none other than the Director of Intelligence at the Air Ministry, so he was apparently untouchable no matter what he got up to. By working for the RAF Ferry Service, he could defy his driving ban by flying from base to base apparently unrestricted. Cannon claimed him as his own personal pilot. Given

Scott's status, they had clearance from someone on high to fly in and out of RAF Jurby with apparent impunity, telling security officers they could not divulge why or where they were going – which if the chatter about Cannon is correct, total secrecy probably was the order of the day.

A trawl through Scott's considerable file contains a list of driving offences and fines for driving without insurance and with defective tyres. He is described as "a single man of independent means, of superior education, appearance and address, but it appears he is of an eccentric mentality, self-willed and of morose disposition. He is often in possession of a cheap second hand car, and in this he tours the country, camping out and often not in communication with his parents for long periods."

MI5's main man on the Isle of Man was the aptly-named Captain d'Eggville (prone to long pompous memos). He pointed out at the beginning of April 1941 that he had for months been pressing London for answers about what Scott was up to on the island, but got absolutely nowhere. Cannon and Scott simply referred any officer's enquiries to an RAF Wing Commander in England, or someone "of high office in the Air Ministry."

Scott was without doubt under Cannon's control. If Cannon was a German agent, Scott would have been perfect prey. He had access to significant military information as the main function of his 'Ferry Service', or RAF Ferry Command, was the transfer of new aircraft from factory to operational units. The Command's operational area was the north Atlantic, and its responsibility was to move larger aircraft around RAF home bases.

Despite his military responsibilities however, Scott was a vulnerable character, as is evidenced by his criminal record. Crucially,

Cannon found it easy to manipulate him, as he did many people.

Scott was a complex dashing high society gent with a fragile, deviant side. Son of 'the Hon.' Denys Scott, a landowner in Devon, he was socially awkward. His mentor Dr Cannon was always on hand to fend off any probing inquiries which went beyond casual niceties.

But officers did find out useful information when they made enquiries at Devon Constabulary. A helpful Constable Melhuish wrote back by return of post that Scott, aged 30 in May 1941, was "fresh-faced in complexion, five foot eleven inches tall... (and) had on the 8th July 1940 been found in possession of a car near Wadebridge and under the circumstances he was detained. He appeared on remand, charged with unlawful possession of two automatic pistols and 15 rounds of ammunition. The defendant was found unfit to plead, no evidence was offered and the same date he was certified and removed to the mental hospital, Bodmin."

The RAF security officers who had whipped up anxieties about what Scott and Cannon were up to, were no doubt astounded to read this given Scott and Cannon's unfettered access to facilities. They demanded further information, only to be doubly surprised by the following memo from MI5 in Oxford:

"Further to my letter of the 24th April... I do not think there is anything more we can usefully do about Scott, who evidently believes in Cannon, but it seems to me an ingenious and possibly dangerous set-up by the latter which might afford him access to military information of considerable importance. I do not know how we are to prevent credulous people from telling Cannon things which they should not, except by ensuring that people who might fall for him should not have such information in their possession, which is clearly impossible. Scott, I hope, will profit by the warning to give no military information to Cannon. Yours, J.E. Badeley."

The strong implication in Badeley's reaction is Cannon and Scott were to be left to their own devices – and perhaps the subtext was: 'Leave them alone'. Badeley knew more than he was letting on. A month earlier however, Badeley had written to Captain d'Eggville inquiring about coded telegrams – rather alarming during a war one would imagine – between Cannon and Scott.

In his reply, d'Eggville wrote: "With regard to Captain Scott, the latter was interviewed by the police but refused to give any information about the telegrams, which he said were a Service matter, and advised the Police to refer to the Director of Intelligence at the Air Ministry."

The matter of the telegrams had only emerged because a Post Office official in Douglas, Mr Minnay, a busy man, happened to make a note of their contents. He informed a police officer that he had a copy of two telegrams which had been dictated from Kirk Andreas 208, the first on August 19th 1940: "Conversation made in detail by KA20: Appointment made for air patient late tomorrow – Tuesday and sea patient early Wednesday.. Tried to get you at North Waltham, Hampshire, also South Coast, Submarine channel busy September 13th"

The second was on September 3rd 1940: "Call from Kirk Andreas 208 (Cannon) to Captain Scott (Fulmer 251): "The date is now definite for September 10th for all those points on the map."

What exactly were the two up to when they flew to England on their secret missions, and who in the Air Ministry or Admiralty, or Whitehall, was sanctioning it?

A chap called P.L. Plant of the Air Ministry Security in King Charles Street, Whitehall, wrote to Agent Pettit of MI5: "John Ernest

Dudley Scott... the above named officer came to see me this morning. He explained that he was a great believer in Cannon and in the latter's ability as a spiritualist and hypnotist.

"You will remember I wrote to you on 24th July 1940 when Cannon had apparently 'picked up' a message concerning Hitler's planned invasion date. Apparently Scott at that time was not in the service but was in the habit of consulting Cannon especially with regard to the details of how inexplicable aeroplane accidents (civil aviation) had occurred."

Plant continued: "I understand that Cannon uses the de Puységur method of hypnosis – he has two female mediums, both of whom have received a good deal of medical training. These women are said to be used for diagnosis with Cannon's patients. According to Scott, although they are capable of receiving information concerning technical and military matters, it means nothing to them unless definite questions are asked. Scott explained this as a type of thought reading and clairvoyance at a distance, i.e. Hitler, thinking out his plan of invasion, causes certain vibrations which can be picked up by mediums. This thought tranference is however subject to interference by short wave transmissions and Scott states quite seriously that the Huns, alive to the danger of leakage, have increased their short wave transmissions very considerably.

"I pointed out to Scott that this was a two-edged weapon and would at least prevent the enemy from intercepting the thoughts of, say, our CIGS (Chief of the Imperial General Staff). The whole story is extremely fantastic and I warned Scott that as he was in the service it would be most unwise for him to visit Cannon and put questions to him regarding military subjects.

"As for the interpretation of the telegrams mentioned in your above quoted letter the first meant that August 10th was the probable invasion date, and that by September the area of operations would be east of a line between the north of The Wash and Southampton. As for the second telegram...(Scott said it) meant that the air invasion would take place late tomorrow, Tuesday and attacks by the sea would develop early on Wednesday.

"Cannon had convinced Scott that danger areas were east of the North Wash to Hampshire line, also that the Channel off the south coast would be filled with submarines. The whole thing seems rot to me, but I should be grateful if you would let me know any further details and also let me know if you want anything else done. Yours ever, P L Plant."

The memo highlights not only concerns about Captain Scott's mental health, but also questions about PL Plant's apparent grudging willingness to go along with what Cannon and Scott claimed. It takes him a while to call it 'rot'. Did he reflect a broader and quite commonplace failure to laugh at, or ridicule, the Cannon occult nonsense?

Cannon's hilarious claims about his own psychic skills and those of the de Rhonda sisters seem to get a bit of respect from Plant, possibly because Cannon was a qualified doctor. Plant, like most people in this story, gave 'doctor' the benefit of the doubt.

Mr Plant thought it was all 'rot' in the end, but still he did not call in the men in white coats to put Cannon into a padded cell. He simply advised to warn Scott not to discuss military secrets with Cannon and the de Rhonda sisters, like they were untouchable, but for reasons that could not be disclosed. Scott was working for the RAF Ferry Service, which in itself brought status and a sense of immunity.

It was all too much for Captain d'Eggville, who wanted answers and thought his concerns about Cannon were being ignored – which of course they were: "Dear Plant, I wrote to the War Office on Aug 14th 1940, asking them to check up on Capt Scott. I wrote again on Aug 16th, Oct 15th and Oct 26th and I never got the information for which I had asked. On one occasion, when I asked for information on Capt Scott I was told nothing could be done as I did not have his initials. But I had given his phone number. Later I was told that there was a Scott at this number, but he was not a Captain. To which I replied that it would be unbelievable that two people of the same name living at the same address and phone number were not in some way connected.

"Interesting as your report on the telegrams is, it fails to answer the questions as to what these telegrams were about, and I am wondering how far this man can refuse to answer questions. The telegrams have now been passed to the Air Ministry – seven months after my first enquiry. I am sure that you will see all this is coming a little too late. For it is now possible that this man's house will be requisitioned in desperation, but that will divulge nothing and he may start all over again... Has Scott been searched? Have his premises in England been ransacked? Yours ever, D'Eggville"

Aside from Whitehall officials obviously not co-operating, there had been an RAF requisition plan for Ballamoar on hold for some time. One arm of the military was giving him secretive support, the 'pull' Agent Sykes refers to, while another part of the military is preparing to take his home and clinic off him.

D'Eggville was to continue to pursue Scott and Cannon for many months. It must have been bad for his blood pressure. He thought about writing to the Governor. But what was the point? On one occasion, he challenged Scott and Cannon at the island's airport to reveal their destination when they flew to England on November 23rd 1940, coinciding with a series of heavy air raids mostly on London, various ports and 21 RAF stations or aerodromes.

Cannon admitted, after prolonged questioning, that Scott had flown him to Hatfield "on Air Ministry business". He said this could be confirmed by a Wing Commander Lane-Burslem, insisting that he (Cannon) should not be named as the source of that information.

What was he doing with his own RAF squadron leader flying him around in such dangerous circumstances? Who was this Lane-Burslem man? And what was the truth about Captain Scott?

92

Whilst Scott was definitely a high class protégé, there was another man of much, much greater significance. Once again, we have Douglas Post Office snoop John Minay to thank for this discovery – his eavesdropping leads us to the diary of one of the most dashing 007-style commandos of the Second World War: Commander Sir Geoffrey Congreve, D.S.O., a character worthy of decorating any of the Ian Fleming novels, an author who himself had wartime contact with Sir Geoffrey. Dr Cannon and Congreve were to develop a very close, top secret, almost psychic relationship as they, along with Joyce de Rhonda, investigated the use of telepathy and applications in the battlefield.

His name first popped up in the Cannon file discovered on the Isle of Man. Joyce de Rhonda's close friend Eva Kane confirmed it by accident, his name I knew I had heard before: "Joyce and Sir Geoffrey Congreve were very much in love. They were engaged to be married... They used to dabble in telepathy, all that psychic stuff.

I thought it was all ridiculous, of course it was. They were kidding me." Little did Eva know how serious they were, how on the nail she was.

93

Two o'clock one morning in May 1941, and the telephone rang in a police station in the hamlet of Sulby on the Isle of Man, not so far from Ballamoar Castle. Picking up the telephone at this ungodly hour was Constable Stanley White. Details of the phone call were typed up and a full report ended up on a desk at MI5 in London around five days later.

P.C. White's report said: "When I lifted the receiver, I heard the Douglas operator, a man, say that he had a call for me from London. And then he switched the other party to me.

"A man's voice said: 'This is the War Cabinet, in London! Do you know Ballamoar Castle, Ramsey?'

"I corrected him, and said: 'You mean Ballamoar Castle in the Parish of Jurby!' He then asked me if I knew Dr Cannon. I answered: 'Yes! I have often seen him!' He then asked if I would take an important message to Dr Cannon, and I said 'Yes! But there is a telephone direct.'

"He then replied that he would try to get through directly to Ballamoar Castle. He never gave me any indication of what the message may have been about. The voice (on the telephone) appeared to be that of a very ordinary person."

Little did Constable White know that eavesdropping on his conversation with the War Cabinet, and also on the subsequent message for Congreve left at Ballamoar, was John Minay, who worked at Douglas telephone exchange. The message read: "To Commander Sir Geoffrey Congreve. Report immediately to Whitehall." Mr Minay wrote: "A few minutes later a person giving the name of Commander Congreve phoned from Kirk Andreas 208 to Ronaldsway Airport asking for a seat to be booked on the first plane that morning."

94

Commander Congreve had served in the Navy in the First World War and retired in 1928, only to be called up in July 1939 to run a series of three-week training courses in Plymouth on signaling.

In his early 40s, he was in the Famous Five mould, a baronet with a very black beard and a family seat in Staffordshire, horses in the stables, best friends with Lord Salisbury and seemingly countless other titled people. His journal is full of references to his harsh life at sea and the difficulties of captaining a converted trawler crewed by 'chaps' (ex-fishermen); references to a rich social life, a love of country life and to his doubts about Churchill's and Sir Roger Keyes' leadership.

Sir Geoffrey treasured memories of his father, always referred to as 'W.N.C.' (Sir Walter Norris Congreve V.C.) and his older brother, Billy, who was posthumously awarded a Victoria Cross for extreme bravery in 1916. There were only two other father-and-son duos holding a V.C. each at that time. Very much his father's son, Congreve used his father's old fashioned word 'Boche' to refer to Germans in his journal.

After presenting his final course at the Signals School, Congreve was given command of a group of four anti-submarine trawlers, the Angle, Arab, Aston Villa, and Gaul, which came under the control of the Royal Naval Patrol Service.

And in January 1940, he was naturally excited, as his journal makes clear: "Not too nice with a gale warning! But we sailed. My first day at sea in my own ship – so a great occasion. Found her hard to handle going astern as she kicks so hard to port and one misses the 2 propellers of a destroyer. But eventually got out without mishap and to sea."

The RNPS suited Congreve to a degree. He was a free spirit and the nature of the patrol service allowed his complex unconventionality to manifest itself, as he dashed from battle arena to Admiralty meeting in London with his pet poodle in tow, fitting in bird watching jaunts between raids. The RNPS was not a career path of choice for conventional blue-blooded aristocrats who had no intention of getting their hands dirty. Congreve was not conventional, and he liked a challenge, perhaps not too wild about mixing with 'lower orders', but like a good chap, he was facing up the damned Boche – and his crew when they looked like they were mutinously turning on him.

Congreve was a complex character. Eccentric in a truly English way, he was gullible, and also vulnerable especially because he was – or had been – going through a divorce; like Scott, Cannon found him open to hypnotic suggestion, in fact putty in Cannon's hands.

95

While there were some specifically-commissioned vessels, the RNPS consisted of mostly requisitioned ramshackle, poorly-equipped trawlers crewed by ex-fishermen and reservists, a significant proportion of whom had had comparatively little military training. For Congreve, therein lay the challenge – unruly chaps who could be trained to know what was good for them.

The majority of the crews were reservists, so the RNPS became a navy within a navy. It became known as 'Harry Tate's Navy' or 'Churchill's Pirates'. Harry Tate was an old music hall entertainer who had recently died, and whose act included a car that gradually fell apart around him. Tate's name had been adopted by the Royal Navy and used for the purpose of poking fun at the trawlers and drifters of the Royal Naval Patrol Service.

During the war, the RNPS had 1,637 vessels including converted trawlers, fuel carriers, motor launches and naval seaplane tenders, but about 260 in all were lost in action. A massive number of RNPS men perished in the war, 15,000 or so, including 2,385 seamen who have no known grave but the sea, bearing testament to their huge courage in freezing, cramped and often violently stormy conditions at sea, quite apart from any battles they engaged in, or bullying by RN officers irritated by the fishermen's non-military ways.

96

The Commander's journal gives a vivid, thoughtful picture of his service, starting around Christmas 1939. Not a word about Cannon until August 27th 1940. What is instantly recognisable is how quickly the doctor gets a grip on the commander's mind. Within days, Congreve writes in deferential tones about his new master: "… Dr C says I am making good progress… He is the greatest man I shall ever meet."

Congreve will have succumbed to the doctor, invoking the spirits of his imperial ancestors to come and help him in his battles. At Britain's, and Congreve's, most perilous hour, Cannon quoted to Congreve one of history's great military strategists, Napoleon, whose preferred method of calming himself was described in Dr Cannon's book, *The Invisible Influence*: "Napoleon used to speak of his mind as containing many cupboards. He used to say that when he wanted to think about something more pleasant he used to shut up those particular cupboards.

"It is clear that there are many thoughts in our mind to which the cupboard door gets somehow closed, and these for a time can be recalled by an effort, as one still remembers that particular cupboard; this explains the comparative ease with which some of the cupboards can be searched and hence the subconscious thoughts quickly become conscious."

Such talk comforted and impressed Congreve, who had thrown himself completely into his military life when his family split up. His journal shows how romance had been a closed 'cupboard' to him. And then he met the remarkably beautiful Joyce de Rhonda.

As regards military matters, it is evident Congreve's mental cupboards were jam-packed with irritation over military 'muddle' embodied by failure in a doomed operation at Namsos in Norway in March 1940, and irritation over 'amateurism' in the Royal Naval Patrol Service.

His military boss Sir Roger Keyes and Churchill himself would replace that cupboard of 'muddle' with a new challenge to take up Congreve's mind: the newly-formed Special Operations Executive, in which he was to become deeply involved. It would be one which would be psychically aided by Dr Cannon, in Congreve and Cannon's minds at least.

The Napoleonic 'cupboards' in Congreve's head, romance and psychic warfare, were to become bizarrely and surreally closely associated. Eva Kane, observing as a teenager at the time, was absolutely right.

97

To understand Congreve's relationship with Cannon, the history of the months before August 1940 (the month of Congreve's first stay at Ballamoar) has to be considered, as do his relationships with key players in Britain's wartime history.

May 10th 1940, and there was a febrile atmosphere in the House of Commons. First Sea Lord Winston Churchill was facing up to the feeble appeaser Prime Minister, Neville Chamberlain. Churchill was cheered on by a blustery old sea dog friend of his – Admiral Sir Roger Keyes, M.P. – who shuffled into the Chamber wearing his full Admiral of the Fleet kit and six rows of medals. Military disaster in Norway was what fired Sir Roger's angry shuffle, and it was the final straw which triggered Chamberlain's demise that day. And on the Isle of Man, Dr Cannon was imagining, in his own unique way, that he too was shuffling a little closer to the heart of power in wartime Britain.

Dr Cannon will have been psychically egging on eccentric Admiral Keyes and Churchill in their attacks on Chamberlain. Years after the war, Cannon always claimed to have advised Churchill, but everyone laughed at him behind his back, including Eva Kane.

There is some evidence that Cannon and Churchill were in direct contact. But there was definitely an indirect Cannon connection to Churchill, if only via Admiral Keyes and Commander Congreve.

Keyes was close to Churchill, and Keyes was Congreve's key supporter within Admiralty, offering him senior posts and organising special operations for him. Congreve became very close to Cannon, if not 'under the grip' of doctor. Congreve went for lunch at Number Ten and met Churchill on a couple of occasions. Whether Cannon did ever 'advise' Churchill directly is possible. But Dr Cannon will have had a vision which at the very least was as follows: his believers influencing those in power; leading psychically-charged, soon-to-be telepathically trained forces, as described in his books.

98

The Secret of Mind Power and How To Use It and *The Invisible Influence*, had been written some years earlier. Had he been allowed to, he would have told Churchill and the War Cabinet of their contents. In them, he wrote of psychic forces and their "power to rein in a thousand horses, whilst permitting one to be the dominant leader and guide them, until all the rest of the thousand are in mental harmony with the lead."

In his madness and self-obsession, Cannon will have seen his words in *The Invisible Influence* as a prophecy of the new mystic future he would help prepare for Britain, with the help of Commander Congreve and Admiral Keyes, both of whom became embroiled in his experiments. Seven years before, Cannon had written: "Telepathy as a national asset is proved also through the pages of history. It is shown that the power of the mind of man transcends all else in the world."

Now, having helped determine the Abdication, he would have seen his chance to determine national destiny again was coming closer.

Churchill had been working as the First Sea Lord, appointed by Chamberlain. But one May morning in 1940, Parliament was in turmoil over an unsuccessful exercise in neutral Norway. The wave of anger against Chamberlain would carry Churchill into office.

For in the months before, Churchill, as First Sea Lord, had realised that the German war effort would be severely scuppered if supplies of iron ore for building armaments could not get through the port of Narvik in Norway's far north. He, Admiral Sir Roger and others had devised a plan to mine the seas and block access with a well armed Royal Navy fleet in the Baltic Sea. But the Germans got there first, invaded Norway and seized the vital ports of Trondheim and Norvik.

The British and French governments had agreed in early spring 1940 that they had to take Trondheim to prevent a further German advance north. And so the rag tag Harry Tate Fleet, with Commander Congreve in charge of part of it, was cobbled together. Fish holds became mess decks; nets and tackle were swapped for mine-sweeping gear; asdic sounding equipment was fitted for anti-submarine patrols.

By the time the fighting force got to Norway, there were twenty six thousand of them: sea sick, frozen, frightened, ill equipped, half trained and very young soldiers, all of whom had never experienced anything like the perishing cold. They were dumped in the deep snow and steep cliffs of the Norwegian fjords in the spring of 1940. Max Hastings comments in *All Hell Let Loose* that the commanders on land had been so ill prepared, they had to use Baedeker guide books to find their way round that most difficult landscape. Many were without radios, clear orders, and often without a welcome from the Norwegians. Hardly a model for any later missions. Dr Cannon and Commander Congreve had suggestions for change in mind when the admirals carried out their inquiries into what had gone wrong.

Yet the government had encouraged the press and the BBC to tell the British people to prepare for a triumph in Norway in April 1940. The British in fact found their position untenable within a short time and told the Allied Supreme Council that they were proposing to quit. The French were (briefly) outraged, then went along with it. Their leaders had other worries: this was all happening a few days before the evacuation from Dunkirk, hundreds of miles away. The Norwegians were left with their wrecked fishing villages, burned out oil tanks, deep resentment against the Allies – and the Germans in charge.

This was the subject of the May 10th debate in Parliament, and when Chamberlain asked for and failed to get a vote of confidence, calls rang round the House for Churchill to take over. Leo Amery spat out the famous words: 'Depart, I say, and let us have done with you. In the name of God, go!'

These two bulldogs Churchill and Admiral Keyes – who had also been called out of retirement – were largely responsible for the chaos in Norway. But they managed to turn the situation completely to their advantage. Churchill took his place at the helm a couple of days later – a cigar-smoking 66 year old, girding his loins for as many battles as it took, no holds barred, to win the war. The Admiral was 69 and grateful to have been back in action. According to the Commander's journal, it was rumoured he was 'ga-ga'. But Dr Cannon was poised nevertheless and saw his opportunity to fulfill his destiny. *His* forces of good were at work when King George summonsed Churchill to Buckingham Palace to take over as PM.

99

On that same day, May 10th 1940, when Churchill was voted into power, Commander Congreve was sitting with his rag tag crew, moored in a Norwegian fjord, under fire from German fighter planes, trying to tell himself he was enjoying a dinner of cold tripe eaten straight out of a tin.

It was mostly aboard H.M.T. Aston Villa that Congreve witnessed and recorded in his journal the horrors and confusion of the badly-thought out campaign, where wounded men had to be taken off for treatment on stretchers cobbled out of fir trees and dragged up the cliffs away from the action.

The entries paint a picture of a man totally committed to waging war who actually starts to feel depressed when he is not in the thick of it. Months later, under Dr Cannon and Joyce de Rhonda's influence, all that was to change.

For the time being however, cool-headed Congreve describes in his journal the first few days of the mission in April 1940 to cut Germany's iron ore supplies. In some remarkable entries, as the bombs fly and the machine guns fire, he "enjoys it all", he calls a weapon 'a pet', and is concerned that the fighting could all end up a bit 'tiresome' – and he even deals with the start of a mutiny. "Three planes over, but at Namsos and did not attack us at harbour mouth. Lovely sunset. Tired. A very full and interesting day but I fear it will tell on my crew and ships gradually. I enjoy it all and love my new gun SEALION – a pet.

"Monday. On patrol at entrance and then went to Namsos. No-one in. Alongside and as I stepped ashore, over they came. On patrol when attacked by six bombers. I kept her hard aport and then hard starboard and I think saved her. They gave us a bad time. Erlicon (gun) jammed and ditto Lewis (gun) and down they came power diving.

"Namsos in a mess. Pier hit and many casualties amongst troops. Arab lying there and much shaken. Off down sound. Nearly all auxiliary engines out of action, mostly broken. Rest all minor breaks etc. A really lucky escape. All v. interesting but might become tiresome."

Congreve was right to be worried that the Nazi dive-bombers, the Arctic conditions and the cold tinned tripe had started to take its toll on his crew. "Some of the chaps are shaken. Raid off and on all day not near us. Norwegians clearing out as they think we'll be bombed here. 'Angle' came alongside at 1.30 a.m. saying they would like relief. A grisly hour to contemplate a possible mutiny! Ballard on the key with a revolver and they took it awfully well. Engineers worst. Chief saying he didn't know the job… The others came when they saw I meant it. But it was a bad hour."

Congreve was transferred to Angle. On May 3, Namsos was evacuated, a massive propaganda victory for the Germans who had been better equipped in the Arctic environment, whereas the British soldiers, and clearly Congreve's less experienced crews, were left to soldier on regardless. Coupled with the humiliating escape from Dunkirk at the same time, Namsos was a true nemesis for the British.

But before the Namsos evacuation, Congreve took a moment for reflection and decided the good weather helps the Boche, in words only an aristocrat could select: "Sitting in the blazing sun on a rocky point looking over this beautiful fiord. Not a sound but the sea and a chiffchaff singing and nothing in sight. Yet I've just seen a heavy attack on 'Carlisle' a mile away and earlier saw the 'Bittern' on fire and later blow up. Really it is an incredible world. The weather remains blazing and not a breath of wind or cloud. Really perfect for the Boche or picnicking."

100

The battered remnants of 'Harry Tates' navy didn't return to Scotland until June 12th. On June 20th, at the Admiralty, he was pleased he was in line for a job up north. 'Good, I fancy that.' The 'job' was to be involved in the setting up of the Special Operations Executive training centre in Inverailort. Dr Cannon's most loyal lieutenant was catching the eye of those in power.

As May turned into June after the Namsos defeat, Congreve was invited to advise admirals and captains on what could be learned; they asked him to point out the numerous operational failures. He did so with the country on high alert – the German invasion of Belgium took place on the very day that Churchill took charge as PM. By mid-July 1940, Sir Roger had been appointed as the Director of Churchill's new baby – 'Combined Operations': the commandos. Congreve was earmarked to play an important part.

The idea of commandos is familiar to us now through film and TV, but it was radical in the summer of 1940. Sir Roger's vision was to harass the enemy in a way which the British had spectacularly failed to do in Norway. He brought together teams of officers from the Royal Navy, Royal Marines, Royal Air Force, Royal Engineers and Special Boat Services to work co-operatively to create a commando force which could have more easily dealt with Namsos-style challenges.

Had he been asked by the same admirals to give his views, Dr Cannon would have added that psychic preparation was the way forward; that psychological training could help overcome the bruising and humiliating failings of Dunkirk and Namsos. With his therapies and relaxing treatments for the stressed military, he claimed the Clinic for Nervous Diseases on the Isle of Man was a good investment for the War Office.

Meanwhile, Sir Roger was on a roll and knew how to push for what he wanted – he was after all an MP as well. From his new Whitehall base, Keyes could lobby chiefs of staff, do battle in key committees, and have Captain Scott fly Cannon in from his island power base to compare notes and plan operations.

Five days after Keyes' appointment as director of Combined Operations, on July 22nd, 1940, the Special Operations Executive was founded – one of the most written about organisations in British history. One of the first SOE tasks involved the formation of the auxiliary units, a top secret stay-behind resistance organisation which would be activated in the event of a successful Nazi invasion of the UK: "The Baker Street Irregulars", or "Churchill's Secret Army" or the "Ministry of Ungentlemanly Warfare". For security purposes, the organisation as a whole was concealed behind names such as the "Joint Technical Board" or the "Inter-Service Research Bureau."

The Special Operations Executive training centre was set up far away from all the action at Inverailort Castle in the north of Scotland. Three hundred star officers would run 3-week 'drop-dead' boot camps. All the commando units were trained here in survival skills, armed and unarmed combat, demolition and field craft. Commander Congreve was in charge of the naval contingent because of his special experience in manoeuvring landing craft.

Every three weeks, each new team of young men was greeted at Inverailort Castle by two ferociously fit specialists in 'irregular warfare' – a man called Eric Sykes and his friend Dan Fairbairn. They bawled a welcome to the newcomers from the top of the central staircase before tumbling and crashing down to arrive amongst the startled newcomers in a crouched position, revolver in one hand and knife in the other, ready for combat. These two had learned during their time with colonial hard-knocks in Shanghai Police everything there was to know about combat and silent killing. "If you think our methods are not cricket, lads, remember Hitler doesn't play the game." Sykes, for instance, trained the two Czech guerrilla parachutists who carried out the historic assassination of Hitler's most loyal servant Reinhard Heydrich in 1942. Congreve loved it all: "Their method is undoubtedly wonderful."

The trainees were given lectures in Nissen huts built on an island in the River Ailort. There was no bridge – so they had to wade through the river and then sit through the lecture – the lucky were wet up to ankles, the not so lucky might be wet up to their waists, depending on the state of the river.

They were trained in map reading – those who made more than a five to ten yard error when tested were thrown off the course. They practised stalking, living off the land, using explosives, setting up booby traps; blowing up tanks, bridges and trees. Once a week everyone, Congreve included when he was there, had to run to the top of the local highest mountain and down just to make sure they could still do it… They practised E-boat ('Enemy' boat) assault landings (the Congreve speciality) and were taken to remote places and told to find their way back in the dark, often under fire. Demonstrate less than great keenness and enthusiasm and you were thrown off the course.

101

Black-bearded Commander Sir Geoffrey came to Inverailort at the end of June 1940. He was eager for glory partly because his father had won the VC in South Africa and his brother Billy had died winning one in the Rifle Brigade in 1916, whereas Congreve had so far only managed to get the DSO, leading as we know the converted fishing boats of the 16th Anti-submarine Striking Force to Norway in April 1940.

A popular figure at Lochailort, he set up a course in handling of small boats, teaching raiders to get ashore and back quickly from ships and boats. It became an axiom of commando work that they should train with the actual men who were to ferry them ashore.

In his journal, Congreve described one of the mountain runs and claimed fitness second to none. He buys into the commando concept, but all is not well with his feeling about the mentor who gave him his job: "K (Admiral Knox) and Major South v. worried about Sir Roger Keyes having come in, think him ga-ga... Everything in its usual muddle..." But then the dilemma: "Sir Roger continues v. nice to me but not enthusiastic about a boat landing. He is much aged and I doubt it being a good show."

In early August, Keyes came to Scotland to watch one of the early night landing exercises on Loch Morar. He looked 'frightful' but was still game. The exercise started at one in the morning and he settled down with a flask of coffee and was soon fast asleep. At dawn the Admiral awoke to find himself captured by two noiseless figures, the Polar explorers Andrew Croft and Quintin Riley. 'Splendid attack!' said Keyes in a moment – one of many – straight out of *Monty Python*.

He brought his old friend Admiral Sir Walter Cowan out of retirement to help. 'Tich' Cowan was sixty-nine years old and kept fit by 'riding to hounds' in Warwickshire. Both elderly admirals could be seen in foul weather on wet beaches, shouting, 'Far too much noise! You must do it again!' Congreve wrote: "More than once I helped to change Keyes' clothes, for his feeble hands were too cold to undo hooks and buttons on a duffel coat."

102

Congreve was able to relax for a couple of days at the training centre just before it opened, taking his poodle, named Poodle, for walks, practising pistol shooting, fishing and searching in vain for a crested tit. When it was his birthday, he was happy when a telegram arrived from his favourite daughter, 'Little Ginger'.

"43 today! Am really getting on but curiously don't feel much older. My astrological forecast shows 'great excitements, events following so quickly etc." No birthday greetings from his wife or two other daughters, because divorce proceedings were going ahead – an unhappy background to his perilous activities. He had had no leave since Christmas – and it was now August. He was heading for his first trip to Ballamoar Castle, a life-changing experience for him.

And on August 28th, slightly more than a year since Cannon first arrived on the island, Commander Congreve impressed airport officers, stepping smartly down the improvised ladder from the plane, his gold braiding flashing in the sunlight, carrying Poodle, and greeted by the de Rhonda ladies, by now very familiar to everyone at Ronaldsway. This was light years away from the big boys' playground of Inverailort. "Cannon was pleased to see me, and Poodle was a great success and much admired."

Cannon, in his full Pickwickian attire, presided over his huge dinner table, groaning with wonderful fresh food, and now graced by this English hero toff Sir Geoffrey, who immediately became the centre of attention. Not that the other guests were without distinction: Cannon's Harley Street patients were allowed to visit regularly, piloted by Captain Scott, defying all security restrictions. They included Wing Commander Lane-Burslem who had founded the British Airline Pilots' Association and was on a secret project to do with landing craft; Admiral Arthur Davies, at that time in charge of some aspects of the North Atlantic Convoys, and of course his wife; Lady Naylor Leyland, on leave from her post as governess to the young Princess Margaret; Charles Kearley, whose family company produced air-sea rescue boats and landing craft, and Mrs. Van der Elst, seriously rich inventor of the first brushless shaving foam, and colourful campaigner against capital punishment.

The treatments started straight away, with Congreve relieved to lie down in one of the black painted rooms and listen to Cannon's recorded homilies, try to rid his mind of the constant fear of betraying his men by making a wrong move and the memory of ships on fire, corpses in the water, blazing oil tanks, endless narrow escapes. Not surprising then, when "Dr. C said I've got some results of Norway left."

"Friday 30th Out with Joyce and Lane-Burslems and have talked much. L.B. a fine chap and she too. All have been upset by Dr. C's prophesies not coming off but agree that time is NOT the same to them as it is to us. Any personal ideas he has are still right. L.B. has the deepest faith in it – as indeed I have and he has practical proof having done several big things with Dr. C's aid, notably the reformation of Imperial Airways – a great work. The war has undoubtedly stopped any developments – as was to be expected but one hasn't lost it – just delayed it."

What was the 'it' he referred to? He continued: "(Cannon) took us round his collection – all presents from a wonderful variety of people. Kings of Norway, Spain, Italy, the Grand Lama, Duke of Windsor, and some of the things of really great value. Some beautiful – notably the buddhas and carpets and lamps. He is the most remarkable man."

He seemed to take everything Cannon said at face value: begging the question as to whether Congreve was one of Cannon's old clients in Harley Street or whether he had come for more than a rest cure.

"Sat. 31st Aug. Another treatment in am." Again, it's hard to get rid of 'Norway results', a source of great trauma: memories of the trashed towns, H.M.T. Aston Villa sinking along with the whole crew's photographs, letters, clothes; the look in the men's eyes as they face death. He left his best beloved Poodle at Ballamoar because "Dr. C. forecasts much bombing in London and the South. They want to keep him and he will be happy and safe. Glad to do so. Left in D.H. (De Haviland) machine... with Eric and Mrs. Lane Burslem and Mrs. Brassey, the child and Mrs. A. interesting flight. Had to climb to 3000 ft. to get over a huge smoke cloud 20-30 miles long near Wrexham. Landed at Cosford about 4.45, said goodbye regretfully to the party. A foul journey to Wolverhampton. Home to Chorltey Park, the house built by my father, which I retained, with 50 acres, when Chartley Estate was sold in March 1939. Boche over most nights apparently. We were run in by police for having lights showing."

103

It was the same year that Inspector Kneen had got a search warrant and found nothing at Ballamoar. That autumn brought the police no nearer deciding whether they should march in and arrest Dr Cannon, or pat him on the back for being a highly successful and entrepreneurial conman making money when most men his age were lowly air raid wardens. He certainly had pull somewhere, and more confident he could not be.

Manx security officers were deciding that since no-one took their concerns about The Clinic seriously, they would take no notice of Cannon's boasts that he worked for the Admiralty, and that he had a hotline direct into Whitehall, and that he was developing an anti-submarine weapon. In the vacuum left by indecision, Dr Cannon was able to boast about exactly what he really was up to, but it seems everyone around him assumed he was lying.

Take for instance the copy of a summons in the Cannon file dated October 1940 (for unpaid debts being served on Cannon by Dickenson and Cruickshank of Ramsey). A report describing the serving of that summons ended up on an MI5 desk in the spring of 1941, six months after it had actually been taken to Dr Cannon at the castle. These 'suggestable' officers were not exactly the fastest in the West. But they did offer up some more insight, confirming what Congreve and others saw going on at Ballamoar.

"Accompanying the Peel-based official, Bernard Makin, was the Rev Harry Lamb, Chaplain of St John's. On serving the summons, the two men were asked into Ballamoar Castle where twenty patients, including two admirals, were receiving treatment using 'different devices and healing powers. Makin was shown a room which was heavily padded, Cannon informing him that the mechanism at Jurby Airport would be stopped when he was operating his devices, if the padding of this room did not exist. Makin was also shown into a room illuminated with a blue light which Cannon stated he used to communicate with the Admiralty, as he was employed by them.

"Cannon then put on a record which he stated was of his own voice and that if Makin was to lie on a couch whilst listening he would go to sleep in a short while. Makin informed me that he was standing up in the room at the time and felt very drowsy after a short time. He also informed me that Cannon's two secretaries, Rhonda de Rhonda and Joyce de Rhonda, knew the date of the attempted invasion on the mainland last September and that it was obtained through hypnotism."

104

It took just a couple of hours to fly from Cannon's surreal world to the chaos of war; from a busy, lush green island to cities where the fear of death and invasion were part of daily life, just a short journey in a plane flown from RAF Jurby most probably piloted by the most loyal of Ballamoarians, Captain Scott.

Tens of thousands of German bombs blasted parts of Britain in the latter part of 1940 and the first half of 1941, and so predictions of invasion like those Cannon indulged in will have set hares running as everyday life went haywire. City dwellers in the thick of it ditched daily routine; for some love and lust took its place just in case death came from the sky. They were in search of encounters which became memories taken to graves in urban wreckage, or 'till death do us part' after the war. Journalist and author Malcolm Muggeridge remembered the London blitz as a "protracted debauch, with the shape of orderly living shattered, all restraints removed, barriers non-existent."

With death so close by, many more people were taking risks they would not normally take. Graham Greene described it thus: "Perception traumatised reality. There was something rather wonderful about London in the blitz, with no street lights, no traffic, no pedestrians to speak of: just an empty dark city..."

Londoners had different priorities, and so too did Commander Congreve, a natural risk-taker who stayed for long spells at Ballamoar and flew in and out of London via RAF Jurby next door to Cannon's castle, his head in a new, different place each time he landed.

Even as bombs fell in the distance, he loved a 'wild swim' in the Serpentine lake in Hyde Park. He could practise swimming silently across the 40-acre stretch of water, imagining enemy agents behind every bush, or perhaps ponder his next mission, be that private or professional. When not in London, he faced death in exotic locations abroad. His private and professional barriers, his 'personal' restraint, had been removed, and he was ready for a new encounter. Like so many millions, death could come at any time.

105

Into the void left in his soul by bewilderment with the military, with politicians, and with his ex-wife, came something new which Joyce de Rhonda was to provide, under the tutelage of Dr Cannon. As he travelled to and fro between London, Inverailerot, and the Isle of Man between the end of 1940 and the first half of 1941 – by coincidence the period of heaviest bombing – Joyce and he became energised by how they perceived themselves within the war effort, that telepathy could change the course of the war, and they were obsessed by each other. And that the hand of destiny – that of 'doctor' – was guiding them.

From his first visit to Ballamoar in August, Dr Cannon had gained a foothold in Congreve's head. Thereafter, the foothold fed what began to sound like a determined sales pitch for a sect. Admirals or captains from Special Operations or Admiralty were to varying degrees open to his ideas. Congreve became the politician with a passion doing the rounds, building support wherever he could. He rarely seemed to sleep in the same bed on consecutive nights. Amongst his peers and superiors, his tales of psychic renewal or attempts at telepathic communications in the battlefield were greeted with overt excitement in one place, tepid indifference or active hostility in another, and on occasion, warnings of conspiracies against him. "(Captain) Wooley... met again for supper at Mirabelle and talked late. He is most interesting but v. discreet. On the other hand much is wrong and his criticisms v. fair but most disturbing. Few people can be trusted".

On his visits to London, Congreve strode from gents' club to restaurant to bar, his cap at a slightly rakish angle, small dog on a lead, muttering through gritted teeth to Poodle about 'the usual inefficiency and muddle everywhere'. He met with friends at Mirabelle, the most fashionable restaurant in wartime London; on one occasion he saw David Niven there, a film star who would have played the role of Commander Congreve with great ease. His Mirabelle mood seemed to be determined but chatty, energised by this alternative world which was taking shape in his head, at the head of which was his new guru. He began to canvass, selling the New World to anyone who would listen.

Dr Cannon's quick-fix psychic excitement was addictive and bonded those who experienced it and believed it. After some initial grooming in August, Congreve began to buy into it. During that first visit to Ballamoar he had met not only Joyce, but also Eric Lane-Burslem, whose name had cropped up when Cannon and Scott spoke to RAF security officers investigating Scott. Within a couple of days he was at the Lane-Burslem house near Knebworth. Eric was showing him round the De Haviland (aeronautical) plant before putting on a "most interesting hypnotic séance" with his wife. Congreve commented: "They are a fine pair and 'well on' psychically."

The Lane-Burslems were true 'Ballamoarians' (my description) and often mentioned Cannon's prophesy that the "10th be the day." Despite the awful nature of what lay behind the prophesy, there was quite a buzz as to whether or not it would come true: would the Germans overrun Britain, starting on the 10th? On the 9th September, Congreve was in the capital. It was racked with "a deuce of a raid – ack-ack fire, flames, smoke, a lurid glow." On the 10th, he was kept awake by trepidation as well as "many bombs. Some close.' But then 'no more invasion stuff apparently". So Cannon had got it wrong again.

106

The journal entries for the next month show a shift emerging in Congreve's life priorities away from militarist Keyes and his cronies towards spiritualist Cannon. For instance, here he wrote his journal as he was patrolling late on the 10th somewhere in the English Channel – "we are where things are likely to happen". But when "the 10th was not the day", in his role as trainee Cannon pupil and wannabe Ballamoarian, he lamented the Cannon prophesy failure and became depressed, then "very depressed" – to the point of confessing to his diary that the RNPS men were not his cup of tea – probably a bit rough and ready and not really his sort of chaps: "Quite frankly, I do not like being at sea, these ragtime shows and strange crews are a worry. I doubt their value. Talbot had obviously lost interest when I talked on phone yesterday." Talbot was a vice-admiral – the youngest since Nelson – and Congreve needed his support to move his psychic matters on. He was needy and vulnerable, and he would show himself to be so again and again in the coming months.

For some weeks later, he again appeared to be going off the boil waiting for his next operation in the summer and autumn of 1940. Little was happening on his psychic battle front either. "I wish they'd call the whole thing off. Bored stiff." Congreve, man of action, trapped in inaction in a "foul place (Chatham). My misery may be down to the weather…rain and cold…and the guns don't work… phones and telegram useless. Was there ever such a game?"

As if to compound his sense of failure, one of his favourite colleagues Lieutenant Richard Stannard, who captained 'Arab' during the Namsos raid, was awarded the V.C. for outstanding bravery during the Norwegian exercise. "I must be the only chap who's done something – without a medal".

By December, Congreve was actively doubting Sir Roger's suitability for the job as director of Combined Operations: "He has shot his bolt long ago..."

Sir Roger wanted him to go on an operation in the Mediterranean. Congreve telephoned the doctor and took his advice: "Don't go". The endless delays and cancellations caused by Churchill made Congreve angry: "The thought of 2 months in the Glenis with no action was enough to put me off…What a disgraceful thing it (the delays and inaction) has all been. Have ever politicians and staff made a greater mistake or showed more weakness before? All this work and good spirit wasted. D-d moral cowards, the lot of 'em." Congreve was on his way to becoming Ballamoarian-in-chief.

107

Adventure on the high seas may not have been as exciting, but glory, he thought to himself, may yet be found in telepathy lessons with Joyce at Ballamoar. In the spring of 1941, it was the perfectly exotic location – huge palm trees bordering a canopy of beech, elm and ash trees, two huge buddhas standing guard at the front doorway. As winter turned to spring, the 'castle' was all the more magical, framed by carpets of snowdrops, daffodils, and rhododendrons.

Dr Cannon was to bring 22-year-old Joyce and 43-year-old Sir Geoffrey together for a specific project – a chance to change history, they told themselves. But no-one else was to know other than the very top ranks of Admiralty and possibly Churchill himself, a man who was to speak of 'the empire of the mind' as a tool of social control after the war.

But other factors played their part too – Congreve's attraction to such a beautiful woman; his hurt middle-age pride at home and in his career; his resentment at being overlooked for medals. She realised she had made a great impression on Sir Geoffrey. Her master, the doctor, was happy she was developing a relationship with him. The secretarial work was handed to Rhonda, and the running of the domestics was taken over by two good capable cooks who had run small hotels in Ramsey.

Joyce was delighted, enjoying being taken into the confidence of a powerful man, someone who she understood to be on the edge of making history. She had landed the prize at such a tender age. Her sister Rhonda had stolen the limelight from the outset in 1936 by being Dr Cannon's psychic diagnostic medium for so many rich and powerful people, including Edward VIII. Joyce had simply been a secretary and housekeeper.

She had seen Congreve intermittently since August 1940. By October, Congreve was totally smitten but had yet to make a move on her. Her one letter and random entries in the diary now held at the Imperial do indeed paint a picture of a woman who is mature and sensitive beyond her years: "Joyce de Rhonda. Aged 22, Oct. 16, 1940. An attempt to sum up one of the most beautiful natures I shall ever meet. She is absolutely unspoilt in any way. Her yoga training has developed her mind and lifted her so high above normal humanity that one views her sometimes with awe, like a traveller in an awe inspiring scene where each turn shows newer and greater beauties. To show her extraordinary powers – which only become apparent when one knows her well. This is a true story.

"Sent to the post office to retrieve a letter wrongly posted and important, she asked for it but was refused in the sorting office. Going back to the counter, she picked her man and without a word willed him to go and bring her (against the rules) that particular letter from among many others. How many powerfully-willed men could have done this? One can only guess at her powers. Yet she remains completely simple, can think no wrong of anyone or feel any unkind thought and in some ways uneducated.

"She must literally be one in a million. Her voice is of great softness and physically she is most attractive and arresting. Happy indeed the man she may love and who would attain all he would desire of life. For she would of her great love and passion reach down from her great height and help him. And there would be no limit to the psychic powers he would develop by her love and teaching. Together (but he always the weaker and the follower) they would become a great force for good in the world."

Having set out his feelings in private in his journal in October – and his position within their relationship – by the following February he had become that man who he himself predicted 'she may love'. In his journal he mentions encounters with her '*which cannot be described here*'. Whether they were top secret psychic experiences which proved them capable of telepathy, or whether they were sexual encounters, he never discloses, but both seem likely. A gent never discusses such matters – even with himself in his own journal. Cannon always said telepathy was more possible when love became a physical experience.

The 'psychic' phase of Congreve and Joyce's relationship began in earnest in February as well, when he spent two weeks at the clinic. The fact that his eldest daughter was not much older than Joyce may have been justified in his mind as his relationship with her was part of an official secret mission. All part of the war effort, of course.

Dr Cannon became the master, Joyce the beautiful tutor, Geoffrey the pupil, the shared mission between the three: telepathy, the evolution of their intense relationship the inevitable consequence of such science, boosted on an 'astral plane' by real love, so the thinking went.

It would be actively fostered by the doctor, its applications as a weapon against U-boats would inevitably emerge, so he predicted: 'You can tune into a mind like a radio can tune into radio waves. A mind creates vibrations. I can tune into the vibrations of Hitler's brain.' Perception and reality were blurring; they were trapped in his world, one which was described and recycled again and again in his books and lectures.

"Oh, telepathy!" Cannon wrote, in *The Invisible Influence*, "...thou Great Master of Destiny whose influence can be felt everywhere!"

Hypnotism he argued was a powerful form of telepathy which might better be termed a 'psychic state'; "...it is as it were the opening of the door into the library of the mind."

During the Indian Mutiny of 1857, "mental telepathy was in full force with these adepts, and the position of the English troops was known to them long before the electric wire had transmitted the information to those concerned. The Government were baffled as to how this information was obtained... They had in their grasp the Master of Destiny, that great Invisible Influence which makes kings reel on their thrones, before which armies stand aghast, so great is its power."

There is no doubt Congreve and Joyce will have heard the same story from Cannon, as will the military men with their English colonial roots who were also close to him. He knew how to push the right mythological buttons, even though the sun was setting on the British Empire.

108

The failure of the Namsos campaign had left its mark. There was pressure for a military success. Congreve had picked up on what Sir Roger Keyes was up to – planning a new Norwegian attack. Cannon and Congreve were going to ensure this operation had a bizarre new dimension 'which could change the course of the war'. Keyes had made utterings he might have known what that was.

Hoping to learn how to put telepathy deployed against the English in India to the same use against the Germans, Congreve and Poodle travelled on February 2nd 1941 to pick up the Steam Packet ferry to the Isle of Man out of Fleetwood. He had said his goodbyes to fellow commando trainers at Inverailort who had also been busy training and preparing for the mission ordered by Churchill and devised by Keyes, Operation Claymore. He would be a different commander of commandos, a fully fledged Ballamoarian, by the time final planning for the operation was underway.

In a strong North East gale on the Irish Sea, he would normally have been depressed and miserable, but now he was coming to see the doctor and Joyce for a longer, mind-expanding spell at the castle and he had a renewed sense of purpose.

Joyce picked him up from the Steam Packet boat at Douglas harbour, and the fledgling couple returned to Ballamoar where a meal was enjoyed as was "a warm welcome from Dr C, same for Poodle. Many people here: Davies (Admiral) and daughter Mrs Wickstead... A Ramsbottom, Mrs Waller, Major Waller…", and Congreve was early to bed. Congreve's chest had been treated with rays, which he said upset him and kept him awake. "The diagnosis was that toxic poison's moving and under control." The next day his chest was clear. "V. interesting!"

Like all Ballamoarians, the commander and Joyce were lectured about the efficacy of love-fuelled telepathy, the benefits introduced to them by 'doctor', as if he were the leader of a sect. In Joyce's words, they 'discovered by accident' that she and Congreve were capable of telepathy, as if it came as some sort of surprise. Her own correspondence reveals there was, unsurprisingly, renewed purpose in what he was doing, or if you are trying to be posh as Joyce was, he had renewed purpose in what 'one' was doing: "Practised daily and improved rapidly. After a few days, he could pick up long messages accurately. Also during this period, tried Astral Projection. This requires hard concentration, the end result being that the person one travels to sees and eventually even hears one. This was very slow at first with little success."

Despite his commander status, Congreve was gullible, appearing to believe anything Dr Cannon claimed. His diary includes abbreviations for certain people. He describes the doctor telling him for instance that he (Dr Cannon) was not popular with people on the Isle of Man as they did not understand what he was trying to achieve and why so many 'high-ups' like 'Ld L' (Lord Lytton) and 'C' (Churchill? Probably not!) came to the clinic. (He refers in his journal to people by the first lettter of their name without disclosing who he was actually talking about.) Dr Cannon was never more than a few minutes from his next opportunity to big himself up.

"G. told Dr C that H had said he reckoned C and he were the only two big men in Europe! Twice sent bombers to have a go at him but weather bad and a big blow put 'em off.

"Wednesday – had a morning treatment and walked in the PM with Joyce… good telepathy in the evening... Am progressing well. A wire (came) to say that I should report to Inverailerot on the 17th."

Military planning for Operation Claymore was underway, so when the wire came on the 5th of February, he knew his time was limited to two weeks, but his tutor and master seemed pleased with 'progress'.

Throughout these two weeks, most of his journal entries begin with "a good morning of telepathy", a mention of who he ate lunch with, and then experiments or exercises, and a moment in which 'doctor' asserts his power amongst his Ballamoarians with a reminder of who their mystic master is: "Feb 10th: V. fine and bright wind cold. Morning telepathy good. 6 correct out of 6 tries (trees, paving stones etc.) Morning treatment and walked for half hour. In p.m. cycled to sea and then walked quite a long way on the beach. Most pleasant.

"Tea'd with the Kanes back by 6/30 for a relaxing exercise. Another experiment at night failed. My fault. Dr C told Captain... that he had produced papers in which he had written a warning. A good proof case of his power."

"Feb 12th: Telepathy has improved... This morning J (Joyce) came to my consciousness, I thought of 1. smoke from the hill; 2. the bridge over the stream by the house. 3. the fighters (planes) we saw standing (on the edge of Ballamoar) .

"All these I got, and downstairs with everyone talking. Sitting near her I 'got' her turquoise instantly. Also pretty good as things going. It is wonderful... we did an evening exercise together – very far advanced (I feel) very optimistic… I am very happy here. More so than I have been for years and more... Obviously I must go back to the war soon but even that will not upset me.

"My physical health improves daily, as do apparently my other powers."

Congreve was top of the class, the best ever Ballamoarian pupil. On the top of a page in his journal, like a school boy he drew two stars exactly like those on the black ceilings at Ballamoar. On the lower part of the page he describes looking with Joyce at the ruins of an ancient cottage in the Manx countryside. Was he imagining them moving in together? Getting married?: "Feb 13th, a lovely sunny day. A.M. treatment then a walk with P and J in p.m. J. and I set off to look at the house Sulby way. A terrible state of dilapidation. A great pity as the outside is good and charming. Beautiful garden could be made but house would have to be rebuilt. Up the camp hill behind and v. pleasant. An evening exercise. Relaxation improving but a long way to go! Young Davies arrived. Lt. R.N. a quiet boy.

"14th Feb: Dull and still but spring like. Some telepathy but I still can do little sending. Walked a bit and all delightful.

"16th Feb: Gone v. cold but we walked…Each day much the same and I could want for nothing better. Dr. C. gave me a beautiful little djinesha. The girls say it is an honour. J's dreams re. the boy are delightful."

Like many thousands of couples in the war, Joyce and Sir Geoffrey had to face what could have been their last moments together. He was going off on another very dangerous mission, so bidding farewell could have been the last time they ever embraced. But for this couple, it was not quite as final as that. They were going to stay in touch telepathically. They had agreed to attempt to predict in handwritten letters what the other was thinking at that moment and to send the predictions to each other.

109

In his other life, Sir Geoffrey had in the months up to February trained his commandos in Scotland, and then had two weeks off. He was to lead them into battle on the Lofoten Islands in the north of Norway. This was to be a highly significant mission for Admiral Keyes and Churchill too. For lots of reasons other than strategic fundamentals, they would be praying for success for Congreve and his men. But would glory come his way because of the 'occult supervision' that Nazi-sympathising history researcher John Gastor claimed – as it turned out – to be focused on Congreve?

As he psyched himself up to leave Ballamoar, he pondered his lust for glory. It was a big motivation for Congreve; such thoughts triggered ponderings of his ancestors, and that would lead him to think of another obsession. He was a 43-year-old baronet who was in great need of a new wife to bear him a son. As things were, if he were to die on this mission, his title would die with him. He had three daughters and was separated from his wife and, as he psyched himself up for Lofoten, he had in his great coat pocket a letter from Joyce. Would she bear him a son if he survived the war and if they married?

Another Ballamoarian Captain George Drummond had done exactly that – married a much younger woman who produced a son after a first marriage had only produced daughters.

For now though, he had a mission to complete: "17th Feb: A sad farewell. J. drove Poodle and I to ………and we left at 11.30. V. cold and bitter wind. And I find I'm to go (to Glasgow) via Belfast."

Once he arrived on his vessel the *Queen Emma*, he settled down in his cabin, and out came his journal once more, his love for Joyce and dependence on Dr Cannon for approval very much in evidence. He was vulnerable and needy as he felt like he was being sidelined by Admiralty: "18th Feb. Ship anchored as gate closed so I'm now 24 hours late! But not my fault. Looking back over this fortnight, can hardly believe it's real. So greatly has life changed for me. I'm so little worthy and of the marvellous future (with Dr Cannon) which is ahead.

"I can't write much here as it is still a secret, but leaving Ballamoar is like going out into the cold night from a warm and happy fireside. This is mostly due to J. of course but by no means all, as there is a wonderful sense of safety both mental and physical there.

"Dr. C, J and R all combine for this. He is of course the greatest man I shall ever meet. Continually one is astonished at his powers and stories. Badly wounded in France, burned by shell bursts at least twice and for 36 hours in one case and the only survivor due to his Yoga. He is above all petty concerns, minds nothing of criticism and remains calm and in some ways simple. He was a Major General (medical) at end of last war and still a colonel M.O.? Has Grand Cross of Belgian, Italian and one other order."

110

Vast tanks brimful of fish oil were the incentive to carry out the attacks on the Lofoten islands in March 1941. From fish oil you can make glycerine; from glycerine you make high explosives. Blowing up fish oil factories in Nazi-occupied Norway therefore became a top priority for both Sir Roger Keyes and Winston Churchill too. Success would be a welcome shot in the arm politically and for national morale. All of a sudden, Norway's cod fishing somehow became connected to the development of the SOE war-waging model if it went well. And that would be good news for Dr Cannon as well as Congreve.

The raid was to target four ports and destroy the fish oil producing factories. Congreve's naval vessels were to capture or sink any German shipping or Norwegian vessels working for the Germans, and to provide naval gunfire for the landing forces.

Lofoten is an archipelago of islands well into the Arctic Circle which has been for more than 1,000 years the centre of great cod fisheries, especially in winter when cod migrate south from the Barents Sea and gather in Lofoten to spawn. The pointed peaks of the chain of islands look like a wall some 100km long and up to 1,000 metres high when viewed from the side. From elevated points around the town of Bodø, or from the sea, visitors delight in the fantastic scenery during the 24 hour sunshine of the summer. In the winter, it is a frozen hell.

While waiting in Glasgow for the order to sail, Congreve telephoned Joyce, although he had failed to 'visualise' her the previous night. He had to leave Poodle in Glasgow with Rosie, one of his lady dog sitters, and he slept aboard the Queen Emma: "I had a good sleep and a 'vague' idea that J. came".

The commandos and their vessels started gathering at Scapa Flow in the Orkneys on 21 February 1941. Bird-watcher Congreve spotted some small exotic birds while the 'Boche' flew high above them. They remained there for almost a week. He landed on Orkney one morning, and had "a jolly day. Nice to be away and out of ship."

A letter written by Joyce reveals how much she was hoping that they would be able to communicate during this mission: "I have a vague idea that he came (telepathically) but it was not so clear as I wanted it."

Before leaving Scapa to head for battle at the Lofoten Islands on March 1, he received *a "delightful letter from J. which promises great things,"* and his vessel departed at 11.30 at night, where he was awake most of the night before a watch at 4 in the morning. He said he felt sorry for the troops on Faroe Island as they passed it, then they took "a zig zag course and it was cold but time didn't drag as it used to years ago, I've got so much to look forward to."

What Churchill wanted to happen was perhaps 'the great thing' which Joyce was to predict for Sir Geoffrey. Admiralty 'high-ups' were watching throughout, from start to finish, as was Dr Cannon, who via Joyce was ready to describe himself as psychic supervisor – as long as everything went well.

Communications with the War Office seemed to be better on this second raid a year on from Namsos, because they heard that a "German Naval Force is going north. Hope this won't put us all off. We are supported by Home Fleet. Cold and beastly…and hope we have a bit of fun tomorrow".

111

Entering the Vestfjorden they were surprised to see all the harbour navigational lights illuminated, which they believed to be a sign that they were not expected and had achieved complete surprise, as Commander Congreve records.

"4th March. Boat stations at 0500. Very clear and all the Lofoten coast in sight. A bit of swell and had a job getting off and then engine wouldn't start. However 1 and 3 got off and followed. Bitter cold and I was a mass of ice quite soon – glasses useless and frozen.

"A very fine scene with the early light on the snow and a huge fishing fleet putting out. We got in safely and landed... No sign of opposition luckily as we were too cold. 3 came in too and then I shoved off and went round the main channel hoping to avoid shipping. But nothing there on landing quay and all quiet."

He was captaining a crew of commandos from all walks of life – many of them had never seen such a dramatic landscape, apart from during their training in Scotland. This was their first mission to Norway, and it was in a place all the more beautiful in golden early morning sun. Some of them were Norwegian fishermen, who in their previous civilian lives had regularly come to plunder the massively rich fish stocks off that stretch of coast. But now they were battle-ready, and on deck in case they were spotted by the Germans. But when no Germans appeared, no-one was more surprised than Commander Congreve, and he was no doubt conveying that peace in the sun back to Joyce.

He blinked and squinted in the sun, he was struck by the beauty of the landscape against the gloopy calm of the sea now disturbed only by a huge fishing fleet. Strange to think there was a war on, yet all was so apparently peaceful in one of the most fortified sections of Europe's thousands of miles of Nazi-occupied coastline.

As they neared the landing quay, there was still no sign of any Germans, despite the fact that some hours earlier, the fish oil factories next to the quay had been blown apart by British sappers. The battle-hungry aristocratic Commander was disappointed. "Seemed very glad to see us. Sappers destroyed a lot of C.L.O. factories and plants and old reservoirs but no one seemed to mind. I walked to end of island. Snow deep and very cold but bright."

Not only was Congreve keen to satisfy the aims of Operation Claymore at Lofoten, but he was on his own private, and very secret mission with Joyce and his master Dr Cannon, but he could tell no-one.

As he leapt off the trawler on to the quayside he was distracted from considering these extra pressures on his shoulders by the vigorous hand-shakes of Norwegian fishermen delighted to see the Brits, and their suggestions of how to expel the Germans. Would some of them like to come back to Britain to fight? While they pondered the suggestion, the wiry, black-bearded commander of commandos strolled off along the quayside, his glasses thawing in the warmth of the rising Norwegian sun.

"Confess to great disappointment in not having any fighting but it would be unpleasant in this cold I suppose. Searched one Norwegian ship but found nothing to warrant a sinking. No Germans or Quislings but brought off 30 or more recruits".

He called at a post office, welcomed like an old friend. Still no "Boche". He bought some stamps as mementos: he would look back on this moment when the war was over – casually purchasing stamps from a post office in Nazi-occupied territory. What a great boast to savour in London's Empire Club.

Little did he know that later that day, March 4th, further up the coast, there was glorious bounty, endless potential for glory: a German Enigma code machine in the hold of the German trawler *Krebs* which had been holed below the line and was sinking. It was a find just in the nick of time before the icy waters swallowed up the vessel. It would allow code breakers at Bletchley Park to get to work and help essential supply ships dodge U-boats in the Atlantic. A massive result for Operation Claymore, but for a downbeat

Congreve, disappointed at not seeing any action.

"Very tired for some reason. The cold I think. Other parties much the same story. Sailed and set course south. Saw one Boche a very long way off and fired at him about 3 p.m. So once more I am disappointed again."

The force that landed at Stamsund destroyed the Lofotens Cod Boiling Plant. Two factories were destroyed at Henningsvær and 13 at Svolvær. In total about 800,000 imperial gallons of fish oil were set on fire; 228 prisoners of war were captured and 18,000 tons of shipping in all was sunk, so the mission had a high propaganda value.

The men under his direct command missed the capture of the Enigma machine – that success was claimed by others – but the glory was ultimately shared by all who went on the raid.

For his part, Congreve only got to shoot fleetingly at some passing aircraft in the distance and drop a depth charge on a suspected submarine. But that did not appear to matter. The Enigma capture and the mission statistics represented all the success Churchill could have hoped for. Dr Cannon – and possibly Sir Roger too – made claims about Congreve's telepathic adventures in Norway, and could bask in that glory, as could Congreve himself, had he wanted to. But given his state of mind, he probably recoiled from any crowing.

"7[h] March 1941. A blue sky and fine following wind. Into Hebrides. We got into Greenock at 6 p.m. and found Sir. Roger and Sec. to meet us. Eventually up to Glasgow and I to dine with them and Bill Haydn. They all seem pleased. Told to go to London but had no uniform so caught 10-8 to Stafford."

Joyce meanwhile wrote in a letter to his daughter, after his death, what she claimed to have been picking up from Congreve's brain on

February 26th, her not knowing when he was in battle: "I dreamed of an orange which turned into a golden sun shining on a snowy place with mountains near. He was there with other Naval Officers and men. He looked very tired but happy. We checked the date and time later and found that he had at that time been trying to tell me where he was. The orange being an old joke between us and a trick to try the powers of telepathy.

"About this time he was very depressed about the lack of excitement at Lofoten and felt that the men resented his being there. Also unsettled about work and lack of real job. No success with A.P. (astral projection)"

Given the significance of the Enigma find – and the fact that the Blackshirt internees on the Isle of Man had heard mention of the Lofoten raid – there can be little doubt about what Dr Cannon claimed: that the success was down to him and Joyce guiding Commander Congreve. Joyce's comments about her getting through to him telepathically and picturing him in a snowy place with sun and mountains (presumably Congreve would not have told her where he was going before he left) and him looking tired but happy would have been construed by Cannon as 'success', as she had not pictured him under attack, but, unusually, in a peaceful, cold, mountainous setting.

The reality of course was different – there was of course no scientific monitoring. It was ridiculous. Joyce was more concerned about her lover's depression, about him being resented by the naval reservists, and about him being worried about his lack of a real job. But none of that will have concerned Dr Cannon, and she will have been swept along by celebrations over the capture of the Enigma machine – and the fact that her man had simply survived.

112

June 27th 1941 I rather regretted not tackling the '26 Champagne.

Commander Sir Geoffrey Congreve, after a dinner with Winston Churchill at Downing Street, June 1941.

Whilst top brass of Admiralty seemed to rate him highly, eccentric claims of a New World will have alienated Congreve from lower ranks. The remark by Joyce about resentment amongst his men, and a perception that he did not have a proper job, would imply all was not well and he was uneasy with his secret project.

Naval reservists were frequently drawn from working class fishing communities. They cannot have taken too well to a toff ordering them around, getting an officer to wave a gun around when they dared question him, as he did during the Namsos disaster, and threatening arrest when they were found to be away from their posts in an incident a year later. After all, he was an aristocrat with a little yappy dog and an overblown sense of his own destiny.

Then comes more reason for alienation from the rest of the world, adding insult to injury if you like, a reason for yet more resentment: in the thick of the war as it was in 1941, Congreve lived the high life for four weeks after Lofoten, left to his own devices at Ballamoar for a whole month. Congreve's explanation? That he was being allowed by the powers-that-be "to perfect his astral plane technique".

An astral plane is described as being a parallel universe, a trance-like plane, almost in a semi-sleep dream world in which verbal communication is not used, just thought transference, or telepathy. When both he and Joyce were on that astral plane, their thought transference and communication would have been described by them as fast and furious, for want of more appropriate adjectives. Amazing and comical as that is, there comes a further bombshell – that he had interest in his experiments from the very top, the 'submarine detection part' of astral communication in particular. (Dr Cannon claimed he and his Ballamoarians were able to 'tune in' to thought 'vibrations' of U-boat crews.) Meanwhile, Joyce was beginning to be integrated directly into commando training at Inverailerot in Scotland.

"April 23rd: Obviously there has been some important reason why I have been left here so long (not recalled to Admiralty in London). Over a month and it can only be that we might perfect a form of astral communication for important use. I think I can say that we have done well and we have worked hard and... Dr. C. says (it) would normally take years to acquire. And I am confident that they will be of some great use to us."

And what has to be recognised here is that far from Whitehall sending in the men in white coats to carry Commander Congreve away, he was invited to Number Ten for a special dinner, and met Winston Churchill, Sir Roger at his side.

113

But in the weeks before the trip to Downing Street, back at what passed as his new home there were no cracks in Congreve's Ballamoarian beliefs. After the demands of the raid on the Lofoten Islands, they took a further passionate twist. Believers claim communication with sexual partners on another 'astral plane' becomes much easier when having tantric sex, and is an integral part of telepathy. That however was "too private for writing". Whether Dr Cannon advocated it is not clear. But when they were not engaged in their private stuff, the training boiled down to 'I' (Congreve) to 'J' (Joyce) telepathic traffic exercises in the grounds of Ballamoar, when sipping cups of tea and eating some of the housekeeper's cake.

"25th March. This has been a terrific week. A lot of it I can't put down but will always remember. No recall from Admiralty so my dear Sir R and W have left me alone. Weather variable – one or two real spring days then cold again. We have walked most days but only one hill climb. Not too energetic.

"Have done a lot of telepathy and it steadily improves tho' I to J is still nothing like so good as J to I which is instantaneous and quite remarkable. We have also done the astral projection every night after dinner. This also is improving and can only be a question of time before she becomes visible.

"The other outstanding (recordable) event is the discovery that J can be hypnotised. But any description of that is also too private for writing. I don't see much of the others here but all seven friendly and pleasant. Poo delightfully happy and v. fit."

Quite why the description of Joyce being hypnotised was too private for writing is not clear. Sex seems the most likely explanation. The process of hypnotising would presumably involve Dr Cannon, raising further questions.

"But of course one must be prepared to go back to war. Any day this time. So much strengthened. Scott came up too, v. nice chap. Doctor C. had all 3 of us in the treatment room and treated J. I've not kept the diary at all but... the more interesting points have been put in the blue book."

The blue book was a bit of a mystery – but its contents amounted to secret stuff he wanted to squirrel away for posterity, probably with an eye to maintaining the family's rightful place in history. When something remarkable and psychic occurred, it was noted in the blue book. His rather noteworthy ancestors and his father were never far from his thoughts, and neither was Joyce when he was away from the island.

114

Were wedding bells about to ring out? Congreve mentions 'rings' – and Eva Kane said they were engaged to be married. And he has something to be grateful to Sir R for – quite what it was is unclear. Was it time off to get married? Their attempts at telepathy continue when they are apart ('Nothing last night'), as do their letters to see if they are guessing correctly what the other is imagining.

"March 12th. To Admiralty with Poo. Bitter east wind and foul. Nothing last night. My appt. not v. good. Saw Sir R. and told him how grateful I am. Did a little work and lunched with Sec. at Fortnum and Mason's. Good fairly cheap, Poo had some too.

"The show is fairly ON (the next operation) – now depends on weather a lot, otherwise shd be o.k.

"I am really a most lucky chap. Mrs Franklin re rings. All J's letters are old ones – alas – at least none since I wrote my two 'difficult' ones. I said to Sir R that I was jolly certain WNC would be delighted at my chance. He sort of looked over his shoulder and said, 'I'm sure he's there all the time, and my old father too.' Rather good. Dined in and bed."

115

Back on the Isle of Man: "23rd March: A most beautiful sunny day. Walked with Dr. C. both girls. Sat out with J all the afternoon and did the letters. Really perfect. Exercise at 6 and a (astral) projection after dinner. Nothing noticeable this time. I had treatment in the morning and talked with R when contacting. Interesting about J. Reports well on my progress."

The fact that Joyce was reporting on Congreve's progress illustrates how Dr Cannon had a controlling grip on him. Joyce undertook assessments of him, meeting them perhaps individually. His firm belief in what he and Cannon were trying to achieve seems almost comical – even more amazing is the apparent official interest in their work not only from Admiral Keyes, but also from Admiral Sir Percy Noble, who was in charge of the Western Approaches during the Battle of the Atlantic. There could have been no-one more important to entice, as far as Dr Cannon and Commander Congreve were concerned:

"Admiral Keyes has been informed of the nature of these experiments and that Sir P. Noble is interested in the idea as regards the submarine detection part of it."

Admiral Noble's work in reorganising escort groups, and revamping escort training methods are widely regarded as having been crucial elements of the eventual success of the Allied navies in the Atlantic battles. From his base in Liverpool he was commander in chief of major aspects of the war effort which kept Britain afloat during times in which the German war machine exacted the greatest pressure through its U-boats. If John Gastor claimed Dr Cannon had 'risen to the top' in some ways, if only by attracting Sir percy's curious eye, this was exactly it.

"Much else has happened but life has been, as regards the outside world and from day to day too lacking in incident to be worth recording. But a most remarkable time."

116

Less significantly but worth noting, Sir Geoffrey is himself remarkable for keeping his feet, in some ways at least, on the ground through his other hobbies: "Cuckoo on April 20th. Willow warbler a day early (seen only) chiff chaff about the same. Weather rather cold and East windy on the whole. No news of anyone as all my letters sit in London but when contacting all are well. Poo v. fit and happy."

But then reality kicks in. He gets an order to go back to London – and appears to get some specific instructions from Dr Cannon. Whether Cannon was involved in military planning via contacts other than Congreve has to be considered a possibility. Contact with Maxwell Knight, MI5's master spy runner, seems a certainty though probably not directly relevant at this precise moment: "30th April. I got a wire ordering me to (travel) yesterday but could not fly till (due to storm) so had another day at B-moar. Cold E. wind. Magnolia covered with blossom, camellias still blooming. And many daffs and bluebells fast starting and a big scarlet rhodo (sic) too.

"Exercises not good but both upset at the thought of departure. Poo knew and wouldn't leave me for a moment. Dr. C contacted and I'm v. well. Told me of some details of what's to be done."

"May 1st: Left at 9.30 and J drove me. We have been amazingly lucky to have had all this time. Flew to Liverpool and walked to

Cathedral. I liked it v. much tho gloomy."

Then comes a hint that Sir Roger Keyes, a pivotal and powerful wartime strategist, friend of Churchill and Conservative MP, was on his own little way to becoming a Ballamoarian: "May 2nd Admiralty at 10 and saw Sir R. His usual good and kind self. He took it well and is quite prepared to believe I can do it.

"Very glad of bed early. A quiet night in then to Inverailort for a conference. Everyone there. A lot of things to do and Commodore made me M.O...

"Again lots to do. Weather cold and beastly but I remain in excellent heart. Letters from J. most days which make a lot of difference.

"Saturday. Practice of various sorts and much to arrange. Beastly cold and nowhere warm in the ship."

Another interesting diary entry paints a picture of the commander putting his foot down with his chaps – of note is how he refers to "them" as "'em". (Presumably his having to speak to the working classes in their own language to make them understand who is in charge.) Also, as landings are exercised with the commandos in Scotland, Joyce assists from afar: "Sunday 18th May. A bad day. I came on watch at 2 a.m. to find no officers and no boats. Got really angry with 'em when they did come and nearly put some under arrest but there were extenuating circs. Exercised landings. J. helped with first... May have made some enemies but I have done my job."

117

Evidence finally bleeds through to Congreve of concern on the Isle of Man amongst MI5 and police officers about Dr Cannon and whether or not he was a German spy. On one of the last occasions on the island before his death, Congreve spoke to Commander Mount Haes, who operated one of the internment camps, who tells him that Lord Granville, brother-in-law of the Queen Mother, was concerned about him, as we already know from the security files.

"Fri. 13th. Cdn't settle but off at 5.30 in a bomber to B'pool. Landed and to Richards who were glad to see me and gave me a dinner and bed. Both v. good. What a frightful place. Sad to leave all at B.

"Mount Haes came to our station and we had a long talk. Governor is worried that various people come and go to B. and he doesn't know who or how... I said money would be found to go... Dr C and I wd go and see Lord G."

Just as there was a build-up in pressure over Cannon, Congreve makes himself available to calm things down on the island, to diffuse tension over doctor's activities.

118

Back in London, and another 'wild swim' somewhere unexpected before heading off for Congreve's crowning moment, 'a very good dinner' with the man himself, Winston Churchill. In this moment, he is with the top brass of the military, his authority on many levels unquestionable – he was after all a titled baronet, a little higher up the aristocratic ladder than Churchill himself. Whilst he may have felt alienated in previous months, he was alongside the most powerful men in wartime Britain. There he was – the man who believed he was telepathic, stood next to Sir Roger Keyes, who also at least appeared to believe Congreve was capable of telepathy, and that the commander was on the verge of translating that ability into an anti-submarine weapon.

Whilst Dr Cannon was not actually at this gathering in body, he was there in mind and spirit. The Nazi history researcher John Gastor had claimed to Blaise Compton in 1985 that 'rather than disappear' after his role in Edward VIII's abdication, Dr Cannon went to the very top of Admiralty. He was absolutely right. Congreve though was cool as ever.

"Managed a quick bathe and then caught 8.45 special at Kings X. Mr. W. Churchill, Gen. Isinay, Admiral Phillips, Sir R. (of course) Martin (P. Secretary) Com. Thompson and self. P.M. asked who I was and was nice about W.N.C. He looks well. A v. good dinner indeed and as much to drink as one cd. I rather regretted not tackling the '26 champagne."

119

As we all know, fact is stranger than fiction, but we also know that all good things come to an end. Did Cannon foresee the demise of his black magic circle in the autumn of 1941 when the triumvirate of Keyes, Congreve and Cannon was dismantled over a couple of months? It would seem not. But why so quickly? Was it by accident or design? Had a Whitehall mandarin suddenly discovered all this witchy stuff and pulled the plug in order to keep it quiet?

After the invasion of Belgium, Holland and France and the Battle of Britain, the early overwhelming sense of urgency was replaced by the realisation that Hitler did after all have weaknesses: that his invasion of the Soviet Union was probably a huge mistake, and that America declaring war would change the course of the war. A rise in British confidence was bad news for Dr Cannon. As was the case for Edward VIII, desperation for the British meant they would do anything to ward off the Germans, and if that meant turning to a master of black magic who might just know something useful, then so be it.

1941 had started so promisingly as he bonded with Keyes and Sir Geoffrey. But as autumn crept in, it all began to slide. One of the three was killed, one was forced to resign amid very public acrimonious battles, and the other was cast into the cold from Whitehall's inner sanctum. And further humiliation awaited those who did not go quietly. Churchill might have been a Keyes ally and a Cannon supporter by default – but there was a war to be won, and he had other things to think about.

The troika's demise began with the firing of a German bullet. Its trajectory on a beach in northern France brought an end to this investigation into telepathy. And like millions of deaths during the war, the outcome was all the more tragic because of what had happened in the days before the firing of said bullet. Love and death go together very effectively in war stories, as millions of families across the world know only too well.

120

In the early hours of July 28th 1941, there was a bit of a swell on the English Channel, and the peace of the sea outside Dover harbour was only slightly disturbed by the chug of two motor launches pulling landing craft with sixteen commandos on board. They were heading for Ambelteuse, on the coast of the Pas de Calais.

'Operation Chess' had been dreamt up by Sir Roger: 12 Commando was to go on an intelligence gathering mission on the Nazi-occupied coast. At the very least they were to assess how much the invasion of the Soviet Union had drained German resources on the French coast.

No. 12 Commando was formed initially in Northern Ireland, a unit said to be based on the tactics of IRA freedom fighters during the war to liberate Ireland from British rule. The commandos were trained at Inverailort in Scotland by, amongst others, Congreve, Fairburn and Sykes, the two who tumbled down staircases and pointed guns and knives at the bottom of said staircase. It was in the capacity of observer from Inverailort that Congreve went along on the operation.

Just two weeks before this trip on the bleak landing craft heading across the Channel, Congreve had enjoyed his 44th birthday celebrations in the best way possible – with Joyce, in the super-modern London penthouse belonging to Charles Kearley, someone else who had taken a shine to Dr Cannon. A wealthy property developer whose family were leaders in the building of air sea rescue boats and airfields, Kearley was protected from call-up into the armed forces. Always an entertaining dinner guest at Ballamoar, very keen on yoga and jazz, he kept a stable of race horses and collected art. He, Joyce and Sir Geoffrey – who also had a stable of horses – had struck up a friendship.

Kearley had bought a farm on the Isle of Man's craggy coast close to George Drummond's residence. After the war, he converted the beautiful house connected to the farm into an elegant hotel where my mother had her first job as a chambermaid/waitress in the summer of 1954, and remembers Kearley bringing 78 r.p.m. records of George Shearing from London and urging her to leave the coffee urn and play the piano for guests in the conservatory. She was amazed by the pictures on the dining room walls – Henry Moore depictions of Londoners sleeping in Tube stations during the Blitz. Along with the other waitresses, she used to laugh at the sight of him standing on his head every morning.

Kearley was a man of discerning taste and liberal attitudes, unlike some others who fell under Dr Cannon's spell. Subject to the wiles of various women guests at the hotel, he nevertheless remained a confirmed bachelor. But seeing the love between Congreve and Joyce, he wanted to make them happy in case it turned out to be the last time they could be together.

He persuaded Cannon to let him take Joyce on the Steam Packet ferry to Liverpool one day in July 1941, and then on a train to London, to the famous Kensal House art deco block in North Kensington, an experiment in social housing which, as a property developer, he had championed with the architect Maxwell Fry. The blank white walls of his penthouse created an ideal space for his marvellous art collection, which was later bequeathed to the excellent Pallant Gallery in Chichester

Congreve wrote in his journal: "Saturday July 15th. Went to Euston to meet them but of course missed them. So to Charles

Kearley's flat. Delightful to see J and v happy. The flat is quite extraordinary. High up and a view right across London through west to south again, very modern and good... a fine space."

A fine love nest too. Keyes granted Congreve leave the following Wednesday, and the three went out and about. The weather was very hot and they went swimming in the Serpentine, then to lunch at the home of Mrs Violet Van der Elst, another long-term Cannon patient. This millionaire inventor of brushless shaving cream had fallen on relatively hard times, according to Congreve: "An amazing lady. Pathetic in most ways. Ruined with money and now down to £5,000 p.a. in lieu of £50,000 or more."

On Congreve's birthday, he was back at work – "office and little else". Then in the evening, presents came: "A delightful gift from J – a bronze Karmakura Buddha, a beautiful piece of work. Most clever of her. From Poo 'a fine silk hanky'," and from the one of his three daughters with whom he had contact, "from little Ginger, a pair of knitted gloves, 'bless her'." This commando leader was in touch with his feminine side, you could say.

Eva Kane – whose family business had become intertwined with Cannon when he moved to Ballamoar – said, when I interviewed her in 2008, that Congreve and Joyce had become engaged to be married. The letter Joyce wrote to Carola ('little Ginger') after the death of her father sets out how she and Congreve had planned a whole new life together, and how practising telepathy had built a strong relationship. The letter also makes apparent Joyce's brave face, sharing deeply-felt grief with the little girl.

121

In his last diary entry, a clue as to Commander Congreve's own politics; a clear hint that he was sympathetic to the imperial old sea dogs who wanted to see an alliance of whatever sort against the Soviet Union. Reacting to the news that America was launching an oil embargo against Japan, Congreve's last ever words in his journal are as follows: "Japan is the latest news. A pity she has wasted all her energy on China or she might have hit those d-d Bolshies hard."

Just before these comments, Congreve discloses that he understands that Operation Thruster – a proposed capture of the Azores against Portuguese opposition was 'dormant'. And in the next moment, presumably he was in the arms of Joyce for one last time, gazing into her eyes as they float on their own sunlit astral plane. Whatever Blitzkrieg mayhem was going on outside, life could not get any better.

122

And then a couple of days later, he was on a landing craft very probably supplied to the British military machine by Charles Kearley's company, chugging across the Channel. Life could have been a lot better at that point, but as long as he believed he was telepathically connected to Joyce, his spirits were lifted.

As a key trainer, Congreve had had little involvement in consultations with the War Office when the decision was taken that the beaches at the mouth of the River Slack at Ambelteuse were to be the reconnaissance point for the 16 men led by Lieutenant Pinckney. In order to take advantage of the short summer night while in enemy waters, the landing was to be made as soon after 0100 as possible, and the time ashore limited to one hour.

The conditions for the raid demanded no moon, a rising tide near high water at Ambelteuse and no appreciable swell or wind on the French coast. The moon and tides were right only on three nights in July, 26, 27 and 28. They chose the 27th. Eye witness accounts gathered at the Imperial War Museum describe events leading up to the raid: it was mounted from assault landing craft towed into position by launches, and then left to complete the 3 mile journey under its own steam, and under the very real threat of discovery and attack by the Germans.

Lieut-Commander Goulding wrote: "It was a clear dark night with the stars obscured by the cirrus cloud. There was rather more swell than expected which breaking on the beach helped to drown the noise of the engines.

"Assault landing craft (ALC) 123 approached very silently and beached about half a mile from position 'P' (the assembly point) at 0154. ALC 73 lying off some 250 yards north..."

Lieutenant Commander Goulding believed they had landed undiscovered, but Lieutenant Pinckney had heard whistles at various points along the coast.

"The party had been ashore for 15 minutes without any sign of enemy activity and the other men were about to scale the cliff when at 0207 a white Varey's light or starshell was fired over ALC 123 from the cliff top and almost immediately firing broke out, a machine gun engaging her from right ahead and rifle fire from each side.

"The landing party returned at once along the beach and quickly silenced the machine gun by lobbing grenades at it but the ALC was being hit by rifle fire and grenades. It was about this time I heard

Commander Sir Geoffrey Congreve say 'Something has hit me' and he collapsed, mortally wounded.

"With the enemy thoroughly aroused, there was nothing left for the landing party to do but to re-embark and by 0215 they were all on board.

"ALC 123 then hauled off the beach... only then was it realised there was something wrong in the engine room; neither telegraph nor voice pipe obeyed. Sub-Lieutenant E Poole RNVR was sent to investigate; he found the stoker (E Booker) dead and one engine out of action. He took charge and in complete darkness got the other engine going in a very few minutes."

Such an ignominious death. Joyce was left broken hearted, Sir Roger and Dr Cannon devastated. All three had invested so much of their lives in Commander Congreve, and two of them had a lot to lose.

123

Old Sir Roger was becoming increasingly eccentric, ranting about his crack commandos. Aside from German bullets taking out the leader of his band of commandos, other forces were working against him. Churchill's support could only last for so long. The dark arts of behind-the-scenes Whitehall machinations began to kick in. The bureaucratic monolith so heavily criticised by Sir Roger was biting back.

Sir Roger's departure from the field of action, albeit not quite falling down dead where he stood, was also a humiliation. Not for him a traditional 'exit' stroll along Westminster's Embankment: a chat with a prime ministerial messenger about 'how things just weren't working out, old chap. How about a trip to the house in the country, a chance to spend more time with the family?' The announcement of Sir Roger's dismissal came not from a government department, but from the UK's best-known news agency, the Press Association, taking even Sir Roger by surprise.

News of his departure triggered interview requests from virtually every newspaper in the land. But whilst the self-proclaimed 'father of the commandos' had plenty to say, he held back for the time being at least. A week to be exact. In contrast to his dramatic contribution to the fall of the Chamberlain government in May 1940, his own exit as head of Combined Operations was rather more low key. At least his humiliation was not quite as public as that which he had helped heap on Neville Chamberlain (many would say Chamberlain deserved humiliating).

The news broke in The Times on November 20th 1941: "Sir Roger has authorised us (the Press Association) to state that he was informed on the telephone yesterday morning by a Press representative, who asked him for an interview, that the Press Association had been informed that 'Sir Roger Keyes today relinquished the important secret work on which he has been engaged for the last 15 months'."

It is impossible to say for sure, but it could be that Congreve's death had weakened Sir Roger a little, but he was already significantly isolated within the military because he was into all this 'weird stuff' no doubt. But he cannot have helped himself if he really had believed Congreve was capable of telepathy. Had he communicated that belief and a number of others, which he doubtlessly did as he never held back on anything, his days would have been immediately numbered. With America looking increasingly likely to enter the war, the desperate measures Cannon

– and by default Keyes – represented had become a potential embarrassment.

In his statement Sir Roger did not expand on his 'secret work'. But he took exception to some of the comments which had appeared in the evening papers, particularly one in which he was alleged to have spoken of the commandos as 'his babies'.

And he did not 'relinquish' his appointment. His responsibilities had in fact been 'withdrawn', and it had happened a month earlier on October 19th, 1941, so the Press Association was four weeks late with the story. The chiefs of staff committee had met and decided to withdraw his responsibilities, igniting yet more anger from Sir Roger who still had the capacity to be a loose cannon. As the Conservative MP for Portsmouth North he raised the issues of 'red tape' in Whitehall, attacking the Government for failing to use the commandos and Special Service troops and the ships, landing craft and naval personnel connected with them, which he had taken the responsibility for training, nurturing, organizing and controlling. He was unceremoniously replaced by Lord Louis Mountbatten.

He complained that 'amphibian strikes' which he had planned had been frustrated by the 'war machine in Whitehall' despite the fact that Churchill was convinced that these troops should be allowed to 'act vigorously' and, in Sir Roger's words, face hazards "to achieve great results which might have electrified the world and altered the whole course of the war".

Sir Roger's comments were directed at the government, but its representative minister in the House at the time declined his invite to rise to the bait, "since that would mean disclosure of information which would … embarrass the war effort…"

His obituary in the Times from December 1945 referred back to this anger in 1941 over his sacking, and that the "weapon" he "had so large a part in forging" was not used or developed further. There was no word on what exactly that weapon was.

Whether the minister's use of the word 'embarrass' referred to anything to do with Dr Cannon or the occult I have not worked out. In the same edition of the Times, the leader comment rebuked Sir Roger for standing up and speaking out in the House. Nevertheless the writer recognised that "these shock troops, in full accord with the Prime Minister, had been designed to fulfill great purposes and had in fact been stifled by a multitude of committees in Whitehall." Sir Roger had drawn a glowing picture of the commandos' potential, contrasting it with the implications of their alleged frustration. He concurred with Churchill's view that Whitehall had a huge 'negative power'.

The Times concluded: "Sir Roger Keyes' gallant and impetuous character has often served his country well, but it may be questioned whether this particular intervention was really serviceable. The right and duty of the House of Commons to consider the conduct of the war are unquestionable... But a Member of Parliament holding – or fresh from – an executive position is bound to be handicapped when he seeks debate upon the subject of his official duties."

Later In 1941, bullyboy Keyes generated even more resentment – but amongst other far less powerful people unable to defend themselves – by criticising the shipyard and dock yard workers who had worked so hard during the war refitting trawlers and ships for the battlefield at sea. They, probably along with many others, saw Sir Roger as anything but the "gallant" man described by The Times. Quite rightly, they bitterly resented Sir Roger portraying them as work shy.

The attack on the dock workers was a sign that he had safely returned to his previous life; the white flag of surrender had gone up, and he would accept his new status quo and not darken Admiralty's door again but not do it quietly. Imperial grandee Keyes was after all 69 years old, super-irritated and lonely, the war being the last proper military hurrah for him and his kind in which Britain was a world power.

124

Congreve was dead, Keyes was sacked, yet it seems Cannon had not predicted that legal moves were already in motion to evict him from his Manx castle. His suspect status had become too much for the RAF security police to bear. And the island's gang of aristocratic internment camp commanders were convinced he was a German spy, and would attempt to convince anyone who would listen to them. If it meant travelling to London to personally lobby the head of MI5, Sir David Petrie, then so be it. That is exactly what they did.

Petrie must have known far more than he was letting on about Cannon's telepathy project and it's supposed anti-U-boat applications, but he let them continue with their campaign. Dr Cannon, dealing with the likes of MI5's spy runner Maxwell Knight, saw himself as a cut above the camp commandant lords.

Charles Henry Maxwell Knight OBE, known as Maxwell Knight, was an English spymaster, naturalist and broadcaster, whilst reputedly being a model for the James Bond books. If Cannon was part of a network dealing with a vast array of people in the military and security services like Scott; if Cannon really did have a hotline to Admiralty; and if he was vetting fascist prisoners as Gastor's interviewees said he was, then he would have had contact with Knight, for a time at least, which would have indeed made him feel he did not have to answer to anyone.

And there was of course the possibility that he could have threatened to expose all the insider knowledge he had accrued not only about the Duke of Windsor, but also about countless other establishment characters. Cannon's head was crammed full of dynamite scandal for which any editor would have given his eye teeth. That probably gave him the confidence to act more than a little arrogantly in the eyes of those around him.

"He was his own worst enemy," recalled Eva Kane, seventy years on. She was aware that the sisters de Rhonda despaired of Dr Cannon's instinct to wind up those who were suspicious of him: "He knew everyone thought he was a German spy, he did not do much to dissuade people, and would laugh about it."

Sir David Petrie meanwhile left the internment camp lords to get on with their little local worries about Dr Cannon. Perhaps he saw the bigger picture: the great potential for blackmail of the government by Cannon. All was calm for him at least as long as Cannon was working secretly for the Admiralty.

125

The internment camp commanders might have been right, but it is unlikely. The possibility that Dr Cannon was indeed working for the Germans can never really be discounted, but it is very slim. There is a slight chance that he may have been a long-term 'sleeping' agent, set up by the Germans in Harley Street in 1935. Dr Doris Odlum, MI5's unofficial agent, herself pointed out an unexplained eighteen month gap in his GMC medical records when he was apparently earning no income from medicine. How he had got hold of enough money to set up his business from scratch was always a source of speculation.

Even in March 1942, well after the 'Dr Cannon issue' was deemed to have been sorted, there were continued concerns: "He is a potential danger on account of the secret information he obtains from certain of his patients." Those words from CID in London, not Admiralty. Was that lack of communication down to cock up or Cannon being protected?

The protection theory wins every time. Someone powerful somewhere in Whitehall wanted him to carry on doing what he was doing despite the fury of island-based officers. Even when, in November 1941, Dr Cannon was accused of claiming to telepathically diagnose from the Isle of Man an air raid warden in Beckenham, Kent, he was not struck off.

At a hearing of the General Medical Council, Dr Cannon was said to have hypnotically treated the warden, a long-term patient of his, over the phone and diagnosed a problem with his nervous system. There cannot have been any hearings like it before or since: Dr Cannon's book *The Invisible Influence* was trawled over, containing as it does references to Yogis of Tibet and his invention, the psychostehokyrtographymanometer, used he said to gauge whether two people were in love. Reference was also made to the fact that he had been sacked, then reinstated in 1933 at Colney Hatch. They also reported that he had offered to perform the Indian Rope Trick in the Albert Hall – but only if someone paid him £50,000, as he had to import his yogis from Tibet as well as buy special sand, and have the hall heated to tropical levels. Dr Cannon was rapped over the knuckles and no more, remaining registered to practise as a doctor for the rest of his life.

126

But in early 1941, there had been a bolt from the blue, a warning: he was made aware that eviction from Ballamoar was a distinct possibility. He took the threat seriously, but not seriously enough. He lapsed back into mocking those who questioned him. He was working for Admiralty after all – why should he take any notice of local security services?

The process to evict Cannon from Balllamoar had started in secret in July 1940, when the search warrant was issued to Kneen. For the coming months a game of cat and mouse was played out. As long as his brass-neck Yorkshire confidence held out, and as long as his protector protected him from on high, he was the cat, local security officers the mice.

But suddenly the RAF wanted him out as they felt he was physically too close to the Bomber Command aerodrome at Jurby, too friendly with the pilots as well. Get that man out, the RAF concluded, and they would requisition the castle and use it for their own.

127

Hidden away, however, in the depths of Whitehall (or was it Downing Street?), the Cannon believers were pulling strings. Obeying orders in April 1941 was MI5 agent J E Badeley. He was the next officer into whose lap the Cannon file fell. He was one who wanted to make his mark. He became obsessed with Ballamoar intrigue, but was definitely pulling his punches at the same time. Perhaps he was playing a clever game of double bluff to keep local officers guessing. Good fun for Badeley, all so very top notch, as the top brass were watching so closely.

On April 24th, 1941, Badeley wrote a lengthy response to Isle of Man MI5 manager d'Eggville's repeated attempts to get answers about Cannon out of Whitehall. In truth, answers were never going to be made available: "I quite agree with the hampering effect you mention of not getting answers with regard to SCOTT and CANNON... It is totally unacceptable that this has gone on for so long."

John Ernest Dudley Scott, just to remind ourselves, was the young aristocratic eccentric who had latched on to Cannon from his seemingly loose attachment to the RAF Ferry Service despite a lengthy record of petty criminal offences.

Badeley's memo continued: "As regards Scott, the Air Ministry have been requested to ask him officially for an explanation of the telegrams from Cannon. But he refused to give any such explanation to police. I think it is worthwhile pressing for this explanation although I expect that SCOTT has long ago informed CANNON that inquiries were being made of the telegrams."

His message to d'Eggville is clear – whilst Cannon may be a problem, and he even acknowledges the spy theory, there is nothing MI5 can do about him: "Dr Cannon is undoubtedly in a position to pick up items of military information of importance, but as long as he is in business, with the kind of clientele he has, I do not see how that can possibly be prevented.

"Dr Cannon, as well we know, is an unscrupulous liar and a rogue but there are difficulties about regarding him as a German agent. If it is suggested that the Germans provided the capital before the war to establish him in luxury in his present castle, it represents a considerable investment for a benefit which could not be estimated in advance. (But…) ten persons at 20 guineas a week is over £10,000 a year, and even half of this is a handsome return on an investment of a few thousands especially if he is able to reduce or escape income tax by being domiciled on the Isle of Man.

"Cannon's only practicable means of transmitting such information to the Germans would be by wireless and he would have had to have made these arrangements long before the war started. If he has such a set, it would have to be very well concealed. Considering the trappings of his house, a most exhaustive search would probably be necessary to have any chance of finding it."

128

Oxford and London-based officers actively discouraged police and agents on the Isle of Man from taking any action. But on the island, officers' attitudes were hardening. By June 1941, customers requesting copies of Dr Cannon's hypnotism treatment gramophone records were being checked out.

And internment camp commandant G St C Pilcher barked questions in memos about Rhonda and Joyce: "Are young women being called up in the Isle of Man? I cannot imagine that the occupation of medium is one of national importance. Have the two ladies registered, and if so, when are they due to be called up? I am sure the governor would like to take a personal interest in this!"

But then on August 8th, a hint of a more interesting line of inquiry. The chief constable Major Young discovered that Prison

Commissioners in Southport had a record of Dr Cannon as being 'in prison' on March 29th, 1941. From Major Young, yet another inquiry to officials in England to find out whether on that day Dr Cannon was "an inmate or a visitor – and which institution..."

Perhaps that was the trigger for what happened next – a complete reversal of dithering and indecision. Just like Sir Roger's departure, it was sudden, an excision, as revealed by a copy of a teleprint on August 18th from the War Office to Western Command HQ, and then to the Isle of Man: an order to requisition Ballamoar Castle, handing over the premises immediately to the RAF who were responsible for all costs involved and works done.

"Action should be taken by the commander, Isle of Man garrison, in conjunction with the Government Secretary, Isle of Man, and the result reported to this HQ in due course."

The result was that Dr Cannon had no choice but to go, demanding compensation of £14,000 "and not a penny less". The removal men were called in. Ballamoar was emptied of everything including Cannon's king size four poster bed and RAF personnel stationed next door took it over.

He was told that he had to be out by October 1st, along with his two ladies. In the event he was gone sooner. One removal man recalled that Dr Cannon was literally turfed out with nowhere to go until a millionaire living on the island at Billown Mansions in Castletown took pity on him and took him in. Some much smaller clinics continued at Billown and later at Laureston Manor in Douglas, but the glory days of Ballamoar were over. Sir Geoffrey had died on July 28th; Dr Cannon was ousted from his castle by September; Sir Roger had his responsibilities 'withdrawn' on October 19th, and left denying he had ever called his commandos 'his babies'. How the mighty – who might have 'electrified' the world and changed the course of the war – had fallen.

One removal man, Fred Moore, recalled: "The furniture? I had never seen the like of it. It went in storage in Ramsey until he could find something more permanent. The two massive buddha statues outside the front door were strapped to the footplates on the van. It looked very strange, the van lop-sided with the weight, driving away into the distance."

129

It was an undignified ending for a clinic which had taken two years to put together and which had seen people with the most fascinating wartime stories gathered around the huge table, enjoying the best wine and food on the Isle of Man, served by two sisters who had shed their identities, like their master, and adopted new names and fraudulent aristocratic titles.

Never again would there be such gatherings, such an eclectic mix of the rich and famous, the military, commando trainers, admirals, businessmen and titled aristocrats come together for New Age-style therapies whilst war was waged. For a significant proportion of patients, death was a very real prospect as they headed off on their dangerous missions. One of the missions by a Ballamoar included Operation Anthropoid on May 27th 1942, the mission to kill Reinhardt Heidrich, one of the most powerful and dreaded Nazis.

Somewhere, locked away in files in Whitehall, are the missing parts which would complete the Cannon story – such as exactly who sanctioned his work and looked after him so well.

It was not until after he had been thrown out of the castle that the head of MI5, Sir David Petrie, commissioned an inquiry into Cannon to establish once and for all whether or not he was a spy. And the inquiry was headed by Major John Frost.

Frost had distinguished himself in Operation Biting, a raid to dismantle and steal the radar dishes or components of the German Wurzburg radar at Bruneval. With Dr Cannon, his modu operandi was "making himself thoroughly acquainted with the man and his methods", concluding some time later that he was not a spy after all. In a letter dated November 24th, 1941, Major Young, the head of the Manx Police, assured Sir David that Major Frost had come to this definite conclusion.

"May I say that whilst taking no active part in Major Frosts's actual investigations, our conclusions, based on material available in the past three years, are precisely the same as Major Frost's. Needless to say, however, should anything tangible ever come to light, we will act promptly. Meanwhile, following Major Frost's interviews with Dr Cannon, I propose having the latter at my office where I will warn him frankly of the possible consequences of any future suspicious conduct."

130

Suspicions of a different kind were what brought about another ending for Cannon meanwhile: accusations that he had been abusing Joyce de Rhonda, and possibly Rhonda too. After Commander Congreve's death and a period of mourning, Joyce began another romance, once again with a military man, high-ranking and very striking, according to Eva Kane. This man was someone who not only articulated the gossip which was rife around the Isle of Man and within the military too, but he also acted on it.

Eva Kane was not unsupportive of him despite her denials that Cannon was ever involved in anything inappropriate with the de Rhonda sisters: "Her new man looked like a film star, probably David Niven I would say. He swept Joyce off her feet. You could tell they were in love. But he didn't like Dr Cannon. He did not like what he was up to, or what he thought he was up to. He thought it was suspicious, improper.

"One night he came round and there was a blazing row, and he said to doctor: 'You can do what you want, but you're not involving Joyce anymore. I don't want you anywhere near her.' He said to Joyce: 'Come on, you're coming with me.' And that was that." So ended another key part of the Cannon story.

Rhonda stayed. Eva spoke of her losing a lot of weight towards the end of her life, unusually so for a woman who had been plump for most of her years. She seemed morose, depressed towards the end of her days. Rhonda, and Joyce's replacement, a woman called Freda, and the doctor share the same plot in the graveyard in Onchan, overlooking Douglas bay. They died ten years apart. There must have been a strong bond between the three of them.

Joyce went on to have children and a happy married life away from Dr Cannon and his mysticism. She and her husband travelled the world. Whether she and Dr Cannon were ever in touch, Eva was not so sure, but she did not think so. It was a fall-out from which there did not seem to be any retrieval. Eva nodded, and was clearly happy for her, but was sad for Rhonda, a life trapped perhaps.

131

Like so many Whitehall-ordered 'inquiries', Frost's was possibly a whitewash, a diversionary tactic to make the outside world think that the publicly-known issues with Cannon were being dealt with. Enough, possibly, to divert attention away from just how seriously his telepathy and other projects were being taken, and so possibly save Churchill's blushes, or more likely those of Sir Roger Keyes. In truth, the powers-that-be knew exactly what Cannon was up to – if they had seriously suspected him of spying and had wanted to ransack his house and question him, they would have done it. Any reliance on an 'inquiry' seems ridiculous, though typically Whitehall, where it is assumed most British 'subjects' are stupid.

Governments have long had form for investigating the paranormal and then denying they ever did it. Jon Ronson, author of *Men Who Stare at Goats*, describes as much in his book about the US army's investigations into the paranormal's military applications. The title is a reference to the attempts to kill goats by staring at them, part of lunatic CIA research into powers which could be used against enemies like the Soviet Union, a regime which itself carried out similarly lunatic work. Whilst the CIA's 'goat staring' has been exposed, the Special Operations Executive had few connections of the Cannon kind, apart from odd characters like an astrologer called Louis de Wohl.

The story of how SOE hired him as a secret weapon against Hitler is disclosed in documents released some years ago. De Wohl moved to Britain before the war and wrote a number of books on astrology, including one he called 'Secret Service of the Sky'. Once again, fascist internees had proved to be useful when it came to identifying potentially useful mystics, as they had told MI5 about him. De Wohl was a man with another kind of past too. One MI5 officer observed de Wohl "claims to have often frequented cafes in Berlin in feminine attire".

132

Mediums and psychics attract influential and wealthy people like bees to honey, or is it the other way round? Dr Cannon was very much crafted by the new media age of the 1930s and 40s, but also by Britain's history and politics at that time.

The interwar years were very much a playtime for the imperial rich, only a few of whom understood the sun was setting on their empire. They had modern trappings of central heating, cars, planes and luxury liners, but still had servants and the power of Victorian industrialists. They could still go shooting on safaris in the colonies and do virtually whatever they liked without fear of comeuppance. Their attitudes and beliefs in the supremacy of all things English had yet to catch up with the modern world around them, and Dr Cannon knew that. He could exploit their fears of newly-emerging politics by invoking forces rooted in nineteenth century mysticism.

Along the way, he invented his own mythology, and drew on myths of countries occupied by the British, some of which he had lived in. By invoking mystical forces that 'colonial subjects' deployed in the battlefield, he knew what he was doing. Amid loss-of-colony angst, he knew which buttons to press.

Such angst was a strong political factor of the 1930s, especially amongst British fascists and right-wingers who called for a focus on preserving the empire whilst pursuing isolationism within Europe.

People like Cannon and Aleister Crowley – mixing as they did with the rich and famous, and Nazi sympathizers too – were useful to government. Cannon and Crowley (himself working directly with MI5) represented access to people with whom those in government would have found difficult, especially with the fascists during the war. The intelligence services and ministers had to understand what was going on in London and Berlin before the war, and in the internment camps during the war. Agents and their runners frequently had politically deviant pasts of their own, so they will have definitely warmed to Crowley and Cannon. Most importantly, they will have protected them both if they had to. Such mystic occultists were taken far more seriously in those days.

MI5's spymaster Maxwell Knight had himself held a post in the British Fascists in the early days of the movement, before he rescinded far-right politics, so he said, and became head of Section B5(b).

Knight was a turncoat and began infiltrating agents into potentially subversive groups. Described as 'a right-wing, anti-Semitic homosexual' by Joan Miller, one of his freelance agents, he succeeded in getting his staff, notably Miller herself, to infiltrate the British Union of Fascists. At the start of the war, Knight and Miller's work resulted in a net being thrown around key fascists at a crucial moment, and led to the internment (some on the Isle of Man) of those deemed to be actively plotting to bring down Churchill. Some of them were probably those same fascists interviewed by John Gastor in 1947, Gastor himself moving in homosexual circles as Knight doubtlessly did.

Knight's agents were involved in tracking some of the very people with whom Dr Cannon was involved either as friends or clients. Sir Geoffrey Congreve was himself on the periphery of such circles. He had a working relationship through naval connections with fascists on the danger list.

Major General John Boney Fuller was a famous military strategist whose ideas influenced those of the German Wehrmacht. He was a devout Hitlerian who even went to the Fuhrer's 50th birthday party.

Major General Fuller had a particular reason to bond with Dr Cannon as he was an enthusiastic occultist and mystic. As a member of the far-right Nordic League and a huge fan of Aleister Crowley, he embodied that connection between mysticism and fascism which characterised the early Nazis. He is mentioned in Sir Geoffrey's journal – he came across the 'old soldier' at Admiralty offices in June 1941: "...a great talker.. not very sound."

Another military man on the far right with whom Congreve had brief contact was Major Francis Yeats-Brown, a fan of Aleister Crowley. Congreve describes meeting both Fuller and Yeats-Brown: military men and members of the cocktail set who had joined the Right Club. Congreve wrote: "Y-Brown a queer-looking man. I might like him I think. Says he doesn't know Dr C. I thought he did. Must hear more of Fuller."

Attracted to colourful characters with a bit of history, Maxwell Knight will have found Dr Cannon irresistible for his contacts with such people, for his brash northern style and for his doubtlessly entertaining psychological assessments of contacts they shared. Cannon openly claimed he had a 'hotline' to Whitehall from the Isle of Man; the fascist internees interviewed by Gastor said as much as well.

Dr Cannon was useful for those involved in the 'dark arts' of government. His contact with Edward VIII was a springboard for him. As the threat of invasion increased during 1940 and the first part of 1941, the doctor's mad-cap beliefs made him one of the most likely candidates to be deployed to explore what those at the top of the Nazi hierarchy firmly believed in: the power of mysticism and the occult. Desperation will have spawned unlikely allegiances between government and people who might know something they did not know.

Then, having worked his way into the military, he found believers who gave him crucial support with which he was able to re-invent himself into other roles, notably Britain's grand master of telepathy.

Cannon was a creature of his times, a creation of his own mythology which he crafted to match the social and political times; his turn-of-the-century childhood in an industrial northern city with a preacher for a father; his post-World War One medical and psychiatric training combined with an entrepreneurial instinct to make money; his charismatic ability to dominate. All those factors meant he could inveigle his way into Edward's life, and then into the Admiralty. He needed support from a wide circle of those within government, and those with influence, and he got it in spades.

In many ways he was Britain's Rasputin, but as the Russian mystic discovered in a very brutal way, gurus only have a finite shelf life.

Appendix I

Below are some notes which Joyce de Rhonda made on Sir Geoffrey Congreve's training and commitment to telepathy leading up to and during his 1941 expedition to the Lofoten Islands.

Feb 6th to 17th 1941.

Discovered accidentally that he could read thoughts. Practised daily and improved rapidly. After a few days, he could pick up long messages accurately. Also during this period, tried Astral Projection. This requires hard concentration, the end result being that the person one travels to sees and eventually even hears one. This was very slow at first with little success.

Feb. 17th to March 22nd.

Practised telepathy each night, sometimes with success but other times completely blank. The most successful of these being on Feb. 18th when he tried to send a message during the night to say that he had had a tiring and annoying journey. It was very clear and of course he was delighted when he received my letter confirming it.

Feb. 21st

(Sir Geoffrey wrote in his log 'I have a vague idea that you came but it was not so clear as I want it.')

Feb. 26th

I dreamed of an orange which turned into a golden sun shining on a snowy place with mountains near. He was there with other Naval Officers and men. He looked very tired but happy. We checked the date and time later and found that he had at that time been trying to tell me where he was. The orange being an old joke between us and a trick to try the powers of telepathy.

About this time he was very depressed about the lack of excitement at Lofoten and felt that the men resented his being there. Also unsettled about work and lack of real job. No success with A.P. (astral projection)

A few nights before March 22nd, A.P. started to improve and he saw me several times. Said in a letter that he had a great urge to see 'The old Ug'. (one of his old friends). Then started a period of great happiness which never left him again. Worries that used to upset him didn't bother him now, and even the stuffy atmosphere and loneliness on the ship or in London didn't bother him.

March 22nd

He returned to Ballamoar. Telepathy and A.P. good. Saw something quite definitely this time. Discovered with delight that he could now hypnotise. We also tried to see something in a crystal. All he could see was a succession of sparks and got a headache for his trouble. I saw lots of little things with no apparent meaning but often saw someone whom he decided was you. We found later that he had been thinking about you (little Ginger) at the time, so decided that it was just telepathy after all.

May 17th

He tried a 'steering' exercise at sea which worked well.

May 18th

Exercises good and made two landings. Difficult to do exercise in daylight as conscious mind persists in coming to the fore. During this period he found it hard to concentrate but in high spirits and very happy.

Appendix II

Below is a letter Joyce de Rhonda wrote to one of Congreve's daughters, 'little Ginger', after her father's death.

'(Your father) often dreamed of his father and wanted to develop himself in some way so that he could dream about him whenever he wished.

'From this time onwards the A.P. became so perfect that he could see and feel me and even sometimes hear me. We always confirmed by letter what I was wearing and it seemed that real success in this direction had come. About June 10th he dreamed about Captain Kerr reported killed in the Hood. Said it was so clear that Kerr must be alive. They had a long conversation and Kerr said 'Don't be surprised if we're shipmates very soon, I've got my eye on a better ship for you.'

'The telepathy became alarmingly accurate and the A.P. too. A few days before he went away, we decided that these things are not really psychic but just well developed senses possessed by almost everyone.

'He spoke often of his plans after the war. He hoped that his Mother would live in Cumberland too, as he had a fixed idea that she only had a few years to live and wanted to make her very happy. He said you would come too. Lots of riding and shooting and you were to breed prize pigs (always accompanied by a detailed implementation)

'There were plans too for lots of sailing, even as far as the Mediterranean. A long holiday in Egypt too, and a short stay in Malta to see his Father's Memorial. At least once a day he talked about Billy and you. He described you so well that I knew you before we met. Said he always thought of you in a velvet coat and was always so obviously proud of you.

'He had never been so happy since you were all together. The day before he went away he talked about Billy and his Father and said that he was sad to think that people like them could be forgotten so soon by their friends. He thought that he would be forgotten even sooner, and could count on his fingers the people who would miss him. I think he was wrong. Don't you?'

Appendix III

Was Cannon in direct contact with Churchill too – and did the Prime Minister have a secret interest in the occult?

The thought of Cannon and Churchill chatting over a brandy about Edward VIII's weaknesses, and then the power of telepathy as a weapon in the battlefield, is an alluring but unlikely one. It is however possible that when Congreve had dinner at Number 10, Churchill was fully appraised of Cannon's schemes and 'skill'.

Limited and unsubstantiated internet chatter in fact has it that Cannon was a member of Churchill's 'Black team' of occultists, and that Churchill was obsessed with the occult; that Cannon was 'chief' at Colney Hatch mental hospital, and was involved in a programme to brain wash people to become 'sleeper' agents, or 'Manchurian candidates'. The mental hospital patients were the guinea pigs. Cannon wanted to blow the whistle on illegal activities there, and was as a result placed under house arrest on the Isle of Man for the remainder of the war.

Clearly, Dr Cannon could not be described as under house arrest from 1939 to the end of 1941, and his movements and behaviour reflect the number of reports generated. For instance from March to May in 1941, there is virtually a document a week detailing something Cannon did or said, or a request for information to check him out from MI5, the Metropolitan Police or the War Office.

But then the numbers of documents plummet after Major Frost's verdicts were delivered in November 1941. Then there are odd documents throughout 1942, and then nothing until an angry rant from a disgruntled customer in May 1945.

Perhaps he had received the starkest warning possible from Major

Young without actually putting him in prison – and that the house arrest referred to on the internet came after the requisition of Ballamoar, and Cannon's silencing. Clearly he had really annoyed someone and his protection was removed. He was being punished by the closure of his precious clinic.

But before or even after that, he may have been part of a broader inquiry. During the war the army set up the Directorate of Psychological Warfare, a group of psychiatrists who examined whether mass brain washing was possible, bringing together research carried out at the Tavistock Clinic and the Office of Strategic Services and War Information.

It is known that brainwashing techniques were used by some British interrogators during the war, according to evidence discovered by the BBC. Their methods included the use of drugs, hypnosis and sensory deprivation to extract confessions from suspected spies.

Churchill must have taken at least an interest in the degrees to which governments or nations could control the thoughts of individuals or whole nations. At Harvard in the USA in 1943, he hinted at such an interest in a speech which has in fact great resonance today.

He was attempting to envisage a post-war world in which English-speaking countries would after the war continue to control the destiny of the world following the demise of the British Empire. Mind control (a more subtle cultural and economic domination, or imperialism, rather than the robotic science fiction type) was a much more efficient weapon than military subjugation, he said.

According to Churchill, to control what men think *offers far better prizes than taking away people's lands or provinces or grinding them down in exploitation. The empires of the future will be the empires of the mind.'*

One can only speculate whether or not Dr Cannon formed part of an obsession within the British government to discover to what extent mind control could exist, and if so whether it could be fine-tuned. Unlikely, but you never know. Only the release of further classified documents will clarify exactly how Cannon fitted into the British war machine.

Acknowledgements

In a book like this – written at a busy time of life (to say the least) – there are relatives, authors and organisations to thank or acknowledge, especially my Dad for the original tip on this story and my Mum for many months of reading drafts, editing, and writing up reams and reams of research.

The book would not have been possible without help from archive staff at Manx National Heritage, the Imperial War Museum, Lambeth Palace and the National Archives at Kew.

Thanks also go to Blaise Compton for supplying me with the tape recording of his father and John Gastor, and the additional information and kind help he gave me.

Eva Kane was a great help too in connecting vital bits of the story, and giving insight into the lives of Cannon and the sisters de Rhonda.

The following also provided significant information and background research:

Wikipedia – aspects of history of WW1

Stephen Dorril – *Blackshirt*

Dr Alexander Cannon – *Invisible Influence*

Dr Alexander Cannon – *Powers that Be*

Dr Alexander Cannon – *Secrets of Mind Power and How to use It*

Wikipedia – Colney Hatch Hospital

Roger Woods & Brian Lead – *Showmen or Charlatans – The stories of Dr Walford Bodie and Sir Dr Alexander Cannon*

Wikipedia – de Puysegeur and Dr Lang

Diary of Tommy Lascelles published in the Daily Mail

Channel Four – Plot to Topple a King

Dr Robert Beaken – *Cosmo Lang, Archbishop in War and Crisis*

Wikipedia

Susan Williams – *The People's King*

Max Hastings – *All Hell Let Loose*

The Times and *Sunday Times* newspapers

Anne Sebba – *That Woman*

Hugo Vickers – *Behind Closed Doors*

For more information on titles from Great Northern Books

visit *www.greatnorthernbooks.co.uk*

follow us on Twitter: *@gnbooks*